THE LAST
OF THE FAMILY FARMS

by

JAMES R. BUPP – Ph.D.

CONTENTS

THE LAST OF THE FAMILY FARMS

PREFACE

After I retired from IBM, my wife Jeanette and I moved to Canandaigua, New York, in June of 1999. We both soon found part-time jobs in Canandaigua, she at Wegmans (a growing grocery chain that was started Rochester, New York, by John Wegman in 1916 as the Rochester Fruit & Vegetable Company), and I at Chase-Pitkin (a building and garden supply retail business that was acquired by Wegmans in 1974 as Bilt-Rite Chase-Pitkin, Inc.). When it was announced in the late fall of 2005 that Wegmans would be closing all twelve of its Chase-Pitkin stores in the Rochester area, I began to wonder what I would do with my time.

My sister-in-law, Nancy Bupp, suggested that I leave something to my children and grandchildren by writing about what it was like to have grown up on a farm. And so I began to think about what I might write that would have some importance to my children and to my grandchildren, or to anyone for that matter.

A special thank you is due to my brother John and sister-in-law Joan Bupp for helping me remember some of the earlier dates, places, and events that were a part of my growing years. I have attempted to keep the dates and the events as factual as possible, but this book is based upon memories that have been stored in my mind for over fifty years. The historical events that we remember pass not only through our own personal filter when they occur, but are also subject to modification as they are processed over and over again in our minds.

I gratefully acknowledge Donna Rehm's "History of the Chippewa Church of the Brethren," which she wrote in 2005. Her writing helped me recall my early learning experiences at the Chippewa Church of the Brethren— teachings from the Bible that have stayed with me throughout all of my years.

This book is dedicated to the memory of my parents, Stanley D. and Dorothy E. (Yoder) Bupp. Their union produced three sons, John E., James R., and Sylvan M. Bupp. This writing has been inspired by their faith in God, their lifelong devotion to the care of God's earth and to the animals that live on this earth, and their profound sense of family and community.

INTRODUCTION

My parents witnessed the rise of the Industrial Revolution and the mass production of the automobile and airplane, the first World War, the Great Depression, the introduction of radio and a little later television, the dawn of the Atomic Age, the Second World War, the invention of the semiconductor, the Cold War, the Korean War, and the landing of man on the moon. Yet, they remained faithful to their God and steadfast to their way of life.

After my father passed, one of the newer generations of farmers remarked that with the passing of my father, "the mold has been broken and there would be no more like him." I firmly believe that he spoke the truth, a truth that applied equally to my mother who lovingly toiled to produce the food, prepare the meals, and care for the family. There would be no more like them. And the way of life they had known would be gone forever.

As I began to think about my early experiences growing up on a farm, it became apparent to me that there were four areas that stood out in my mind as being distinct and different from the experiences of children growing up today. Life today seems so different from the way I was brought up as a child on my parents' farm. As you read this, I hope you will understand how life was on a family farm and how those distinct experiences influenced and shaped my growing years, how I dealt with problems, and how I interacted with people. What I accepted as perfectly normal thinking and behavior will definitely seem strange or even abnormal to some of you!

The first distinct difference about my early years on the farm is that we did not have a TV! And the local paper was not delivered until late in the afternoon. So much of what one reads today in newspapers, magazines, or on the internet, or watches on television or on a DVD is of a shocking or violent nature. And it seems that news media attention is only given to those events that are shocking and violent in nature. My earliest recollection of TV was at my friend Ronnie Hartzler's house when I was probably in the third grade. It had a screen of about seven inches on the diagonal and a big thick magnifying glass in front of the screen which made the picture look like it was ten inches on the diagonal! The first program that I watched was *Kukla, Fran, and Ollie,* which was a puppet show. We did not have a TV in our home until around 1950 when I was about ten years old. I started my day without having to see or listen to the news media heralding the latest cases of violence that occurred over night. When I woke up in the morning, I got dressed and did my chores, which were to give some water and feed to the chickens, and then I returned to the house for a nice warm breakfast prepared by my mother. The whole family always had breakfast together. After that, it was off to school, which started with a quarter of a mile walk down the road to catch the bus. My early sources of knowledge came from my parents, my brother, and my school teachers (both public school and Sunday school), in other words, from my very own community, rather than from the news media or the internet.

The second area that was distinctly different was that we ate our own animals and vegetables, which we cared for and grew on the farm. The animals and the vegetables were commodities that were carefully cared for, then latter sold or used to sustain our existence. One just didn't become friends with the little calf or the cute little piglet as they would soon be sold. They were not pets! Nor were the animals we raised abused or mistreated. I have often said that my father took better care of his animals than the care received by about three-quarters of the world's human population. Our farm animals always had shelter, plenty of food and water, clean bedding, and medical attention if they became sick. In fact, my parents refused to raise veal calves or to eat veal, because veal calves are given a milk diet that makes them so weak they can hardly stand by themselves. Such a diet allows the meat to remain white and tender. They were equally opposed to raising caged chickens, which can never go outside to scratch in the dirt for some worms to eat or to get any exercise.

Most people today do not understand or care to know where their food really comes from. If you like fried chicken as I did when I was growing up, you simply go to the grocery store and buy a blister package of chicken parts all neatly cut up and ready for the frying pan. But

I understood fried chicken in a much different way. The chicken that we ate started out as an egg, which had to be incubated and then hatched into a chick. We purchased the chicks several weeks after they were born and then raised them in two small brooder houses that were carefully heated with a small coal stove until the chicks were big enough to be put outside in a fenced yard. At this stage of their lives, the chicks were called pullets. In about six months to a year, the pullets were vaccinated and moved into the laying house. There they produced eggs for sale and meat to eat. After the chicken lived through its productive egg laying lifetime of a year or two, the chicken was sold for chicken soup. And the cycle would begin all over again. If we had fried chicken for Sunday dinner, my mother would select a chicken from the flock on Saturday that looked like it was not laying eggs. One of my tasks was to take that chicken and chop its head off using a hatchet. The head of the chicken was held by two nails driven into an old stump located behind the garage. One swift blow from the hatchet and end of chicken! After the chicken ceased to flop around, my mother would immerse the bird into a bucket of boiling water which made it easier to pull out all of the feathers. She would then singe off the remaining small pin feathers over the fire from the old oil stove in the kitchen, and cut up the chicken into parts. I never felt sorry for the chicken. It was part of a life cycle that I was accustomed to and, besides, as a hungry, growing boy, I loved fried chicken!

Butchering hogs in the winter was another event that I vividly remember. This event was a "family event" as enough hogs would be killed and preserved so that, not only my family, but also my grandparents would have enough meat for the year. January was the month of choice for the annual butchering event. I remember one year when my father killed seven hogs. Now, that was a lot of meat! The snow was cleared in the yard and a big iron kettle was placed over a huge wood fire. A large wooden vat was brought down from the barn. The vat was lined with metal so it would hold the hot scalding water. After the hogs were killed and bled out, the carcasses were dipped into the vat of scalding water, and then the hair was scrapped off of the hog. The hog was hung up by the hind legs on a "teepee" arrangement of poles, and the intestines and innards were removed. Nothing was wasted. Most folks don't know that real sausage is made from ground up scrap pieces of pork meat that are then squeezed into "casings" which were the intestines of the hog. It was my mother's job to clean the intestines of the hog, which she did by carefully scraping them with an old dull knife on a board and washing them in salt brine. We boys used to blow up the hog's bladder, tie it off with a string, and then after it dried for several days, used it as a ball to play catch with!

The fatty pieces of the hog were all cooked and then squeezed in a press, which pressed out the fat. The liquid fat was then placed in twenty-gallon crocks and, when it solidified, it became white in color and was known as lard. The crocks of lard were stored in the cellar of the house. Lard was the shortening that my mother used in all of her cooking. She knew how to make wonderful pies and cookies and pie crusts that can not be duplicated with modern shortenings. After all of the fat was squeezed from the pieces of cooked fat, there remained a solid "cake" which we called "cracklings." My brother and I used to eat some of this by-product like a snack when it was still warm. But mostly it was used as special treat for the dog and the cats.

The farm had a smokehouse, which was used to preserve the hams and the sausage. We would gather some branches from the apple trees in the orchard and my father would start a small fire in the smokehouse. The hams and the sausage links were hung on several horizontal wooden poles above the smoky fire. After the hams were smoked, they were sprinkled with borax, placed into a muslin bag, and then hung from a hook in one of the upstairs rooms. No further preserving was needed. If you wanted a couple of slices of ham for dinner, the ham was taken down and you cut off the required amount of meat with a meat saw. The hams that we buy today in the store have all been pumped full of salt water to make them more tender and to maximize the grocery's profit since meat is sold by weight. But it bears little resemblance to the ham that I used to eat when I was growing up.

My father was the meat cutter, a skill that I never learned, and my mother would can or freeze all of the remaining meat. Some of the small fatty scraps of meat were finely ground and cooked into a "pudding." The "puddin'," as we called it, was preserved by canning and then either served hot or it would be allowed to cool and then sliced into patties, which were fried in a pan. Much of the preserving of food that my mother did when I was growing up was done by canning. Frozen food freezers in grocery stores came into general use around 1940. I believe that we bought our first food freezer sometime after the end of the Second World War.

Raising and slaughtering animals for food was a part of my experience growing up on the farm. And the animals that we ate for our sustenance were all "organically" grown with no growth hormones or other unnatural substances fed to them. The shortening that my mother used to make her wonderful pies, cakes, and cookies was "lard"—fat rendered from the hogs that were slaughtered for meat. No one worried about cholesterol and, judging from the longevity of my grandparents and parents, I would have to conclude that many of today's health problems have been introduced into our diets from our modern, scientifically engineered and "manufactured" foods.

One fall, long after I left the farm, I returned to hunt rabbits with a new shotgun that I had just purchased. I remember shooting the rabbit and then my son and daughter, Michael and Michele, who were quite small at the time, watched as my dad skinned and butchered the rabbit. I watched the horror on their faces as I held the rabbit by its hind legs while my father pulled the fur down over the rabbit's head, and it suddenly occurred to me that they had never seen an animal killed and butchered for its meat! And so it is with most folks living today. But there seems to be an ever-increasing awareness and suspicion over our modern food and water supply as we discover that we have very little control over it anymore.

The third distinct experience of growing up on a farm was that work was not something separate from family life. It was an integral part of life growing up on the farm. My mother didn't drop me off at a day care center before she started her daily routine of preparing the meals, washing the clothes, or tending to her garden. Nor did my father drive me to school before he headed out to the fields to begin mowing the hay or cultivating the corn. Children were expected to do their share of "chores" as soon as they were old enough to carry a bucket or push a lawn mower. As I mentioned earlier, one of my first chores was to feed and water the chickens before I went to school. And after school, there were the evening chores of bringing the cows in from the pasture for feed and water before they were milked. My parents didn't have to take me to baseball or football practice or to pick me up afterwards. I had my chores to do at home after school.

Yet the routine of doing chores, which centered on caring for the animals and tending to the fields and gardens, also brought our family very close together. The family ate three meals together each day that were lovingly prepared by my mother. Breakfast was at 7:00 a.m. after the cows were milked and put out to pasture. Our breakfast consisted of eggs and pancakes and cereal in the summer with fresh milk from the barn. Fried corn-meal mush with syrup might be substituted for cereal during the winter. But each breakfast was always served with fresh eggs and fresh milk. The milk that we drank was not pasteurized and it wasn't until I visited my uncle's home that I found out how strange store bought milk tasted! Our noon meal was called dinner and almost always consisted of meat and potatoes with fresh or canned vegetables from the garden. After completing the evening chores, which started at 4:30 p.m., supper was served around 6:30 p.m. This meal too consisted of meat, potatoes, vegetables, and fruit grown on the farm. My mother prepared three meals a day, seven days a week, 365 days a year for my father, her three sons, and an assortment of cats and a dog, and she never complained. You see, it was an expression of love. She did all of the meal preparation and washing the dishes afterwards as there was strict division of labor between farm women and men: The women raised the children, took care of the house, prepared the meals, and cared for the garden. The men worked in the barn, taking care of the animals and tending to the fields. An exception to this rule was that my mother loved chickens and she helped to care for the chickens and gather the eggs. My father would wash the eggs and pack them into cartons very early in the morning, starting around 4:00 a.m. when he first arose before he would go out to the barn to begin to milk the cows.

And there were no vacations from doing the chores every morning and evening. Not on weekends, not on holidays, or even when friends or relatives came for a visit. The animals had to be fed, the cows had to be milked, or the hay had to be baled. One exception was the Sabbath as my father did not work the fields on Sunday, but the daily task of taking care of the animals went on as usual. Sunday was a time to go to church, and then in the afternoon, we kids might have a ball game out in the pasture with some of our friends or we might go fishing or swimming in one of the local streams in the summer. Sometimes, my parents would use Sunday afternoon as a time to go visit family or friends, or to just rest up from the labors of the past week. But come 4:30 p.m. Sunday afternoon, all family hands were expected to be home ready to begin the evening chores.

The fourth distinct area of life on a family farm was the unique partnership that existed between folks who worked on a farm and the Almighty Himself. When you think about raising your own food, you will quickly come to the realization that there is only so much that man can accomplish himself without the help of a good and gracious God who sends the sunshine and rain for the crops and the green pasture for the animals. And so it was quite natural that farm families had strong religious ties. We were no exception. We went to church each Sunday regardless of whether we felt like it or not. Attending church was not an option. It was the same as doing the chores; it just came with the lifestyle. And the church also played a central role in the social life of the family. One did not just go the church and then leave right away. Folks stayed long after church was over, visiting with their neighbors and friends and catching up on the week's news. For us boys, this was always a painful wait, as we couldn't wait to get home to start a ballgame or some other activity on Sunday afternoon before chores began.

I find it quite shocking at the lengths that today's media, politicians, and public school officials are going to, trying to separate religion from our daily existence.

No, you can't call it, "The Christmas Season," it's the "Holiday Season," or the motto, "In God We Trust," which is printed on our money must be removed as it might offend someone. It's more politically correct to honor Sacajawea, the Indian women who successfully guided the Lewis and Clark expedition, than it is to give God any credit! Is it any wonder that our churches are empty today and that our young people don't even miss going to church as they have never had the opportunity to learn about the church's teaching? Much of what was taught in Sunday school has remained embedded within me. And to my way of thinking, those teachings are much healthier for the mind of a growing child than the teachings of today's news media and the internet. I think that it would be very difficult for a child of today's world to separate truth from fiction, reality from entertainment, and fact from advertisement, which is solely created for someone else's profit. We did challenge the teachings of our school and Sunday school teachers, but most of that challenge came when we were old enough (college age) to do our own thinking and to live with the consequences.

CHAPTER 1
EARLY REMEMBERANCES

I was born January 8, 1940, in a house on the "Funk Farm." That home still stands and is located on Fulton Road about three miles North of Smithville, Ohio. Farms in those days were known by the names of their owners or by the names of the owners who had previously owned the farm. The "Funk Farm" as it was known, was located across the road from Emmit Yoder who was my great uncle. Just to the west of Emmit Yoder's farm was the farm of Fred T. Yoder, who was my mother's father and my grandfather. To rural people, babies were born at home, just like the birth of the animals on a farm. I do not know who was in attendance at my birth. My mother never spoke of it. But I do know several things my mother told me: As a new born, they could hear me breathing all over the house! You see, I was born with asthma, which would plague me during my growing years and was apparently inherited from the

Yoder side of the family. The second thing my mother recounted to me was that we had a puppy dog at the Funk Farm and that dog and I cut our teeth on the same rubber bone as we played under the kitchen table! The

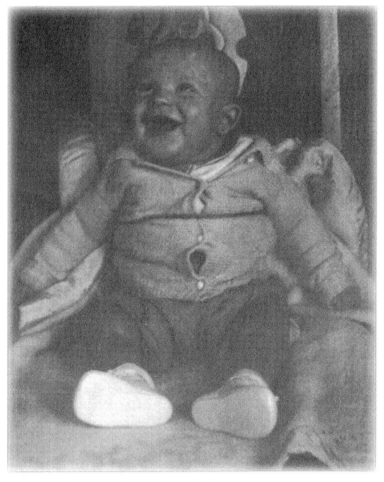

James Bupp, 1942

third incident my mother told me was that my brother John, who would have been five years old at the time, used to take me up to the top of the barn bank in the baby carriage, and then let the baby carriage with me in it fly down the barn bank! I guess that the carriage landed upside down in the potato patch one day and my mother had to clean all of the dirt off me! She also told me that he got a good paddling for that deed! Of course I do not remember this event, but I think it was the start of a long sibling rivalry between my older brother and me, which we frequently engaged in, and continued until the day that he left for the Army on December 2, 1957 when I was a senior in high school.

Our family moved to the Bupp Farm, which was located at 3391 E. Hutton Road, Wooster, Ohio, when I was two years old in January of 1942.

This farm had been the home of my grandparents, Walter George and Emma (Benner) Bupp, having moved there in 1908 when my father was approximately six months old. Grandfather Bupp purchased the farm across the road where he and my grandmother lived until their deaths. Grandfather and Grandmother Bupp slept in the northeast bedroom of the Bupp Farm, which we knew as the "hired man's room." This bedroom was so named because my father hired several men to help him with the farm work when we boys were growing up, and they slept in this room.

For a while, both farms were run as "Walther G. Bupp and Son," but they were eventually taken over by my father after Grandfather Bupp died in 1946 when I was six years old. I do remember Grandfather Bupp, and I can picture him as he came out of the barn one day at his place when they were thrashing wheat. He had a red bandana tied around his neck. In those days, one didn't have a combine to separate the wheat from the straw in the field. Instead, the wheat was cut and bound into bundles and then stacked into shocks out in the field until the thrashers came. The thrashers brought the thrashing machine and the steam tractor that separated the grain from the straw. The straw was either blown onto a big pile behind the barn or stored in the barn as bedding for the animals. The grain was stored in big bins in the barn called the "granary." Later,

the stored grain would be removed from the granary
and ground up at the mill to be used for chicken or

*Grandfather Walter and Grandmother Emma Bupp,
date unknown*

cow feed. In the case of wheat, the excess would be sold on the market for profit.

I remember that Grandfather Bupp was a rather stern man and, one time when I was helping him do some chores, he said that he was going to "fire me." I took him literally and my mother had to explain to me that he did not mean that he was going set me on fire!

Grandfather Bupp passed away in 1946. I remember that he was in the hospital for a short time with some kind of a lung disorder and died while in the hospital. And I can remember the sadness the family went through at the time. As was the custom in those days, my grandfather's body remained in the southwest sitting room of his home prior to the funeral, and I can remember seeing him in his casket. I faintly remember that he was a source of aggravation for my mother (I never really understood why then) and that the partnership between him and my father did not really work out very well. With his passing, my father bought the farm across the road where Grandmother Bupp lived and she enjoyed living there for another twenty years of her life, tending to her garden before passing in 1966.

The family of Stanley D. Bupp with
Grandmother Emma Bupp, 1948

I have my most vivid recollections of Grandmother Bupp as she would always come to the door to greet us boys when we went over to "Grandma's place" to do the chores or to work in the fields. I can still picture her working in her garden wearing her red sun bonnet. As was the custom in those days, women did not drive cars. Neither grandmothers nor my mother drove cars and were totally dependent upon their husbands or other friends to drive them. We always took Grandmother Bupp to town when we went shopping on Saturdays (that's right, one trip a week to the stores!) and she would go to church on Sunday with a neighbor lady, Mrs. Edith Yates, who lived on the farm just to the east of ours. Yes, it seems strange for me to write these words, but my Grandfather Yoder didn't believe in teaching women how to drive, even though my mother did go to college and taught school for one year.

One of my chores was to mow Grandmother Bupp's yard for her. At first, my older brother mowed her yard and then he and I mowed it together. Later on, I mowed it by myself when we had a power reel mower. Before we had the power mower, it was my brother John's job and mine to mow the yard at our place and at Grandmother's place. We used only a push reel mower, and sometimes the grass would get so tall that one of us would have to tie a rope around our waist and attach it to the base of the mower handle and pull on the rope like a "horse" while the other would push on the mower handle from the back. My brother and I would take turns being the horse, but I think that I ended up being the horse more often than not! We would pull and push on that mower until our sides ached and we were ready to drop from exhaustion. I almost forgot about mowing yards with a hand mower until I was driving down Route 96 recently near Ovid, New York, and while passing an Amish farm in the area, I watched three children who were about five years old struggling to mow their big yard with a hand mower, two acting like the horse, and the other pushing on the handle. I guess it's what we would call "Team Work" today! When we mowed Grandmother's lawn, we usually were paid a little money or offered some cookies from her big blue cookie jar that resided in the kitchen cabinet. Toward the end of her life, she had no money to pay me but would instead say "thanks until you are better paid." I have always remembered her for saying that to me, and I have never regretted helping her as it was just one of the chores I did when I was growing up. Children of today's world have become so conditioned to the exchange of money for a service that they will do nothing around the home unless they are paid for it. But when I was growing up, work was something that was a part of and not separate from the lifestyle that we enjoyed.

My other grandparents, Rena and Fred T. Yoder, lived about five miles from our home. They went to the same church that we attended, the Chippewa Church of the Brethren, and we saw them every Sunday at church.

Grandfather Fred and Grandmother Rena Yoder, 1948

My Grandmother Rena was the second wife of Grandfather Fred Yoder, since his first wife Anna, who was my mother's mother had died in 1938. I never knew Anna Yoder, so Grandmother Rena was my grandmother. The home where they lived was the home that my mother grew up in. Grandfather Fred was a farmer and was much easier going than the Bupp side of the family. He did not have a dairy farm, but rather raised beef cows and crops for sale. He was a gardener and a naturalist. I can remember the wonderful garden in back of his house. The tomato plants grew as tall as a person's head, all tied to a series of wooden poles in a "wigwam" type of arrangement. One tomato plant was planted at the base of each pole, then heavily fertilized with some rich cow manure from the barn, and finally covered with straw to keep the weeds from growing and the moisture in the ground. It was a technique that my mother successfully used in her garden and she obviously learned it from her father. The tomato poles were young saplings that my grandfather cut in the woods, which were also part of his farm.

I remember going to Grandfather Yoder's home and playing on their porch and in their large yard. There was a very large weeping willow tree that grew near a small stream that ran under the lane near the barn. It was a lovely shady spot to play during hot summer days, and it was here in the spring that Grandfather Fred showed us how to make "willow whistles" from the young growth of the willow tree. He would take out his pocket knife and cut off a small section of new growth. Then he would twist off the bark in one piece and whittle out the interior wood and replace the bark. It made a fine whistle! We would often go there for dinner and Grandmother Rena would make a huge meal that we all enjoyed. The finale to her dinners was always a hickory nut cake, which had small pieces of hickory nuts mixed into the cake and then lovingly decorated with whole halves of hickory nuts stuck to the entire frosting on the outside of the cake. It was Grandfather Fred who gathered the hickory nuts and then, down in his basement during the long winter nights, he would crack those nuts in such a way as to not break the nut so it could be removed in two whole pieces. Now I have often tried to duplicate his skill but whenever I tried it, I usually ended up with a pile of smashed nut pieces mixed with shells! But he knew how to do it, and those whole pieces of hickory nuts were one of his contributions to Grandmother's dinner. After we had eaten all that we could hold, Grandmother Rena would always ask me, "what can I get for you?" and I would answer "nothing" and she would have a rather puzzled look on her face and then say, "we don't have any of that!" And then we would both laugh!

One of the things that always intrigued me as a child at Grandfather Yoder's house was the crank telephone that hung on the kitchen wall. It was connected to his brother's house, Emmit Yoder, and maybe to the house where I was born. One placed a call by picking up the receiver to see if anyone was talking, and if the phone was free, you turned the crank. All of the phones on the line would ring, but you would know if it was for you by the number of rings, say a long and two shorts. Otherwise, you wouldn't pick it up. When I was child, that phone always caught my eye and I think that it was still in use. The cabinet was made out of oak, and it contained two dry cell batteries and a hand cranked generator which, when turned, generated the electricity that caused all of the bells on the line to ring. When my Grandfather died, I had brother John purchase the phone for me at Grandfather Yoder's auction, and I still have that old phone in my basement. These early phones were the original "internet." But, they had some really great advantages: You owned the phone and the line that ran between the houses. There were no monthly phone bills! And one didn't have to worry about spam or unwanted advertisements. The only risk was that someone else might be using the phone when you wanted to make a call, but since these folks were all neighbors, I'm sure that it wasn't too much of a problem. Party lines were very much in use when I was growing up and our phone on the farm had anywhere from six to ten people on the same line in the Wooster, Ohio, area. Party lines persisted for a long time in rural Ohio, and I didn't enjoy my own line until I held my first job in Endicott, New York, in 1968. A party line also served the purpose of finding out what was going on in the neighborhood and "chat rooms" existed at that time! If you listened to someone else's phone conversation, my mother called it "rubbernecking" and my parents certainly frowned on our doing that. The phone in our house was to be used only for business relating to the farm or for emergencies.

Summer time was a time when the relatives came for a visit and when my uncle Truman Yoder, his wife Patsy, and my cousins came for a visit, grandpa Fred would take us fishing. We would go to one of the neighboring farms. Most farms at that time had a small stream flowing through them and the area where the stream flowed was usually wooded and was used as a permanent pasture for the cows during the summer. It was usually an area that was considered too hilly to be cultivated and was left in a more natural state. At any rate, our fishing trip consisted of finding a likely hole or an area where the creek deepened. We did not have poles. Our first task was to find a tree limb or stick that could be used as a fishing pole. Grandfather Fred usually had some line and some hooks from which we made our own fishing tackle. Next, we would hunt for worms. We would search under rocks or under an old log that might have fallen near the stream. As usual, the group would soon tire of trying to catch a fish and then everyone would go swimming in the creek (nude, naturally). Grandfather Fred would sit on the bank, watching all of us as we cooled off in the heat of an August afternoon. He would just sit there and enjoy the time with his grandchildren. I can't remember us ever catching a fish, but I will always remember those fishing trips!

Sometimes in the summer, Grandfather Fred would peddle fish that he bought from a fishery along Lake Eire. I can remember how he put a large wooden box in the trunk of his car, which would be filled with ice and freshly caught fish from the fishery. After returning from Lake Eire, he would stop at his relatives and neighbors to sell the fish house to house. He had an old poultry scale that he hung from the trunk lid of his car, which he used to weight out the fish. He would have some bass, or pike, or sheephead. My mother would clean the fish, and we would have fresh fish for supper, but I never really acquired a taste for fish as I much preferred the meat of the farm animals that we raised.

Grandmother Rena Yoder was a devoted Christian and we all had to be on our best behavior when we went to her house for a visit. She would love to tell the story of how she would never take a drink of Coke a Cola as she learned at one of the bible conferences that she had attended that they added a little alcohol into the Coke as a preservative and that no alcohol would ever touch her lips! (Our parents never bought soda pop for us, anyway, but she loved to repeat the story.)

Grandmother Rena was exceptionally blessed with good health and she would recount how she never had a sick a day in her life! She did live until she was 95 years old, although her eyes had failed her by that time, but she was truly blessed with good health. As was the custom in those days, young girls were often "farmed out" to live with a relative or neighbor for room and board and a little money. This usually occurred at a very young age as soon as the child was able to do a little house work. Grandmother Rena told me how, at the age of eight, she had worked for $1.00 a week and she thought that she was making good money!

Nothing was wasted on Grandfather's farm. Table scraps were fed to the chickens or the hogs. Old pieces of clothing or coats were never thrown away. One of the things that my Grandfather Fred and Grandmother Rena did during the long cold winter nights was to make hooked rugs. We would probably call them crafts today. I call them works of art. But to them, it was a way to pass the time usefully and to not waste anything. My grandfather would lay out the pattern on some burlap that served as the center or core of the rug, and then my grandmother would cut up old wool coats that she had laid away into very narrow strips of perhaps several inches in length. The patterns would be anything but dull. They were brightly colored and might depict colored fall leaves or flowers arranged in a pattern. The strips would then be woven individually into the burlap and tied off in the back. It took thousands of strips to make a single 3ft. by 5ft. rug! The rug was finished by sewing a boarder around the edge. I can remember that their house had perhaps half a dozen or more of these rugs. I have one that was given to me and, although it was made during the time when my grandmother's eyes were failing her, it is truly a work of art. And being made out of wool, it wears and lasts for a long long time.

Grandfather Fred and Grandmother Rena Yoder were examples of rural folks who lived in the 1800's. They lived a rather simple life and were very devoted Christians. For the most part, they were healthy and enjoyed taking care of their animals and raising their own food. I do remember my mother telling me that one winter they all became ill with the flu during an outbreak of influenza. She told me that they were so sick that my grandfather could not go out to the barn to feed or water the animals. I remembered that story since I know what a cow sounds like in distress and I can hear the cows "bellowing" for some food and water but no one could come to their aid. A lot of people died during that outbreak of influenza in 1918. Grandfather Fred passed away in 1960 and is buried in the East Chippewa Church of the Brethren Cemetery alongside his first wife, Anna (Klopfenstein) Yoder who died in 1938. My Grandmother Rena (step-grandmother actually) died in October 3, 1973 and is buried at the Mt. Peace Cemetery, Hartville, Ohio.

CHAPTER 2

THE FOUNDATION OF THE FAMILY

My mother grew up on the Fred T. Yoder farm North of Smithville, Ohio, with her father Fred, mother Anna, and brother Truman F. Yoder. I have an early picture of her feeding the chickens when she was perhaps four or five years old. We would call these chickens "range chickens" today. She loved to care for the chickens and that love of animals extended into her adult life on our farm where she tended to about 600 chickens that brought in some weekly "egg money" that was used to buy necessary supplies when we all went into town to go shopping on Saturdays. In the photograph, my mother and her brother are shown together when mother was ten years old and Truman was two years old.

Truman F. and Dorothy E. Yoder, 1919

My mother attended a one room school (I believe it was known as #6), which was located about three miles from her home. She walked to that school every day, following the railroad tracks that led her to within a mile of the school, which was located on top of a hill. She would tell me that the older children looked after the younger children, and that they used to sled ride down the long hill during recess. The school house was heated by a coal stove, and the metal chimney pipe that ran the length of the room provided those who sat in the back of the room with a little heat. On cold winter mornings, her mother would take two potatoes and warm them in the wood fired oven and then put them into her mittens. The warmth of those potatoes kept her hands from freezing while she walked to school. If the snow was really deep, she was allowed to ride the horse to school. As she recounted to me, there were times when the snow was so deep that the belly of the horse dragged in the snow as they plodded along to school.

As I have written earlier, my Grandfather Fred did not believe in having women learn how to drive a car, so my mother never learned to drive but had to be driven everywhere she went. And I suspect that it was quite unusual for young rural women to attend college in those days. But I also suspect that the combination of her growing up in a very religious environment and the sheer strength of my mother's will led her to attend Manchester College, which is associated with the Church of the Brethren.

My mother graduated from Manchester College in North Manchester Indiana in 1933 with an A. B. in Biological Science. I would not recognize her from the picture in the year book. She was active in Philalethea (a Bible Society for students who were preparing for Christian leadership), Y.M.C.A., Women's Student Government, and the Choral Society. It was my mother's belief in education and religious training that led me to attend Manchester College some twenty-five years later. In fact, I had the same French Professor, F. E. Reed, and when I mentioned my mother's name, he immediately said, "Yes, I remember her. She sat right over there," pointing to a chair, "and walked with a very determined walk!" At my mother's funeral, she was described as a very steadfast woman, meaning firmly loyal and unchanging in her beliefs. If there were only two words which would describe my mother—determined and steadfast—those would be the two!

My father grew up with his parents, Walter G. and Emma (Benner) Bupp, on the farm where I grew up. They moved there when my father was about six months old in 1908, after having lived on the Benner Farm, which was located about ten miles North of Orville, Ohio. My father was the oldest in the family, and he had a sister Edna and a younger brother Reno Bupp. He attended Smithville High School and was an avid basketball player. In fact, he was on the Smithville High School County Championship Team in 1926. They were called the "Raisin Eaters" as they used to down a lot of raisins to give them a quick burst of energy during the game! We used to have a basketball hoop on the old wagon shed near the barn and another one inside the barn on the farm where Grandmother Bupp lived and we would practice shooting baskets whenever we had a little extra time. My brother John played basketball throughout his high school years but my career ended in junior high as my asthma prevented me from fully participating in the sport. My father was a man of few words. When we were growing up, my father would frequently fall asleep in his chair around 9:00 p.m. as he arose at 4:00 a.m. to start his daily chores. We kids used to get into all kinds of squabbles in the evening, and my mother would caution us not to wake him up because "there would be real trouble!" He was the absolute authority in our home and we all pretty much marched to his wishes. His role was to care for the animals in the barn and to tend to the fields. The responsibility of bringing up the children, raising and preserving the fruits and vegetables for the family, and doing the household chores, which included preparing three meals a day seven days a week, were all left to my mother. I remember one time when I had been using the tractor and disk to prepare some ground for planting and my father complained to my grandmother that the marks left by the disk were not in a straight enough line! My Grandmother Bupp later told me that "he was kind of particular when it came to working the fields," which was quite an understatement! We boys were never allowed to plow the fields with the tractor as we could never plow in a straight enough line to suit my father. But we were taught to work at an early age; I learned to drive our 1940 SC Case tractor at the age of five as soon as my legs were long enough to reach the brakes. That tractor had a hand clutch so it was easy to drive. The summer after I had completed first grade, I was driving the tractor that pulled the bailer when we made hay. My father loved his tractors and enjoyed spending many hours working the fields and cutting the grass in the fields and alongside of the roads, which bordered the farm. When I was in eighth grade, my father bought a Cockshut tractor that he was particularly fond of, and he named it "Little Bertha." He would spend hours and hours mowing with that tractor as it had a hydraulic lift on the mower mounted under the tractor. Taking care of the milk cows occupied most of my father's time as they provided the steady source of income for the family. We milked about twenty-five to thirty head of Holstein cows, a job that had to be done twice a day, 365 days in a year. These animals were well cared for with plenty of food and water and fresh bedding each day. My father named each cow and would call them by name when it was milking time. Each cow had its own stanchion and knew where it belonged. After milking a cow, the milk would be weighed and recorded on a record sheet hanging in the barn. Some of the cows' names, which I remember he used, were Bertha, Molly, Blackie, Sue Ann, Bonnie, and Edna.

I do not know much about the courtship of my mother and father as those things were never discussed in our home. But I suppose that they met in high school. My father was two years older than my mother. The only story that I can recall from their courting days was told to me by my Grandfather Fred. They always knew when my father came to see my mother as he would come down the lane and drive up to the house without shifting the gears in his car. You see, the lane was a long drive down a hill and then rose up a small grade as it passed the barn. My father always tried to anticipate things in advance, so I suppose he went down the hill just a little faster so he did not have to shift gears when the lane went up the little grade and turned into the house.

My mother went to college and graduated in 1933. She held a teaching job at Waynesburg, Ohio (located southeast of Canton, Ohio), during the school year of 1933–1934. It was after her first year of teaching that she and my father were married on June 5, 1934. The reason I know this date is that they were given a mantel clock as a wedding present. This mantel clock sat on a shelf in the kitchen of the old farm house where I grew up and, on the inside of the back door of the clock, my father had written down the date. This clock struck out the hour and also chimed on the hour, half hour, and quarter hour. As was the custom, each person who performed some service on the clock, signed and dated the back of the door when the work was completed. After my father had passed, I was given this clock, and I had it serviced in 1998 by Kyle Dalton, who lived near my home in Endwell, New York. I then gave the clock to my daughter Michele and her husband Aaron Clarke after they were married as a remembrance of my parents and also as a reminder of the slow but steady progression of time.

My mother became pregnant with my older brother John shortly after they were married. And indeed, that event ended her teaching career since, in those days, school teachers could not be mothers and teachers at the same time. I also recall the great sensitivity that my mother had for the timing of my brother's birth, as he was born on March 7, 1935 and it apparently caused some talk about her sexual impropriety, which she staunchly denied! How strange as in our world today, most parents only hope that their daughters get married before the baby comes!

I also know very little about how my mother and father started housekeeping together. The little that I know is that in 1935 they took care of Tracy's Tourist Cabins near Kidron, Ohio, for about a year. My mother would clean the cabins and make the beds. I believe that my father worked in the gas station and a small store located near the cabins. Their wage was about $26.00 per week. My mother recounted to me how my father would "hang out" at the store and have a Coke while she would be working or taking care of the baby. The following year (1936), they would move to the Funk Farm north of Smithville, Ohio, which was located across the road from Grandfather Fred's farm. And it was on this place that I was born on January 8, 1940. In 1942, when I was about two years old, the family moved again to the Bupp Farm.

My youngest brother, Sylvan Merle Bupp, was born on August 13, 1946. The name "Sylvan" came from one of the hired hands named Sylvan Amstutz who stayed in the hired man's room and helped my father with all of the farm work while John and I were growing up. I can remember that mother had a wicker-basket baby carriage, and as the baby grew older, one could move a lever located in the back of the carriage, which would drop the front end of the baby carriage down so that the baby could sit up. Well, one of our favorite tricks was to sneak up on the baby carriage while Sylvan was sleeping and pull the lever on the carriage and he would start bawling and mother would come running to see what was going on. Poor Sylvan, with two old brothers, he never stood a chance!

The lifestyle of living on a family farm and even the vary nature and personality of my parents seem to be best characterized by the old mantle chock that sat on the shelf in the kitchen. My father would faithfully wind this clock every Sunday morning. And he would set the time about five minutes fast so that he would always be on time for church or for whatever required him to be on time. My father's sense of punctuality carried over to me as I usually set my watch about five minutes early so that I too will never be late! When I was growing up, the old clock in the kitchen reminded me when it was time to begin my chores, or when it was meal time, or when it was time for me to start walking down the road to be picked up by the school bus. You see, I never had or carried a watch when I was growing up. However, my father did carry a pocket watch, which he used to remind himself of the time when he was working in the fields or in the barn.

The slow, steady tick tock tick tock tick tock of that old mantel clock also set the pace of our lives. Work on the farm was never done; it just ended at the end of a day, only to begin again early the next day. Most tasks were not completed in a single day. Feeding the animals, milking the cows, plowing the ground, preparing the soil for planting, planting the seeds, cultivating the crops, waiting for the harvest, harvesting the crops, and storing the crops in the barn were part of a process, not just a single event. And this process kept repeating, just like the tick tock of the old mantle clock.

CHAPTER 3
THE ROAD TO SCHOOL
BEGAN AT CHURCH

For as long as I can remember, our family attended the Chippewa Church of the Brethren located near Creston, Ohio. For those who are interested, I have attached an addendum written by Donna Rehm in 2005, which gives a brief history of this church. My Grandfather Fred and his first wife Anna are buried in the East Chippewa Church of the Brethren cemetery located some ten miles to the east of The Chippewa Church. I have often wondered why Grandfather Fred and his first wife Anna (Klopfenstein) Yoder are buried there since they never attended that church, but it is because his wife's family is buried there. In 1921, some of the folks who attended the Chippewa Church of the Brethren broke away to start the East Chippewa Church of the Brethren. Donna Rehm's history does not record that date or the events that lead to the split. The East Chippewa Church of the Brethren was considered a little more progressive than the Chippewa Church we attended. You will note that Donna Rehm did record the fact that, in 1928, twenty-five people left the church after the congregation had voted to install a piano! For all of my growing up years, my Grandfather Fred Yoder attended the Chippewa Church of the Brethren with his second wife, Rena Yoder. In fact, the electronic organ that resides in the church today was a gift from my Grandfather Fred's estate.

Church attendance was part of the weekly routine of living on a family farm. Just like milking cows twice a day, seven days a week, going to church was a natural part of being in a partnership with God. Indeed, according to the creation as recounted in Genesis, the Lord created heaven and earth in six days, and on the seventh day he rested! I never heard my parents say on Sunday morning, "what shall we do today?" After the Sunday morning chores were completed, we all dressed for church. Sunday school began at 9:30 a.m. followed by church services at 10:30 a.m. Church services usually lasted until 11:30 a.m. or later, depending upon the length of the sermon. There were no "nurseries" for babies or small children. Children were expected to stay with their parents throughout the church service, and woe be it if a child became fussy or began crying, as it was up to the parents to remove the child from the service. And from the interior of the church, one would frequently hear a good wack, wack, wack on the child's bottom and the crying would immediately stop! Such was the beginning of the discipline required for a child to start learning how to act and behave during a church service.

I owe a great deal to my Sunday school teachers. They were mostly women who were servants of God and had the patience of Job to work with the children one hour a week to teach young minds about God. There were different classes for different aged children up to and including the youth. The adults met separately. Some of the names of my teachers that I recall were Esther Miller, Ruth Miller, Genevieve Sheets, Esther Boman, Earl Miller, Donna Rehm, and her husband, Jack Rehm. All were people who loved the Lord and cared enough about children to try to help them understand the story of Jesus and the good news that He brought. Genevieve Sheets led the singing of hymns in the Sunday school classes and in church. I have never forgotten the old hymns and, once I hear the melody of an old hymn, the words just seem to come back from nowhere, indelibly stored somewhere in my mind.

Church was more to rural folks than just the teaching of religion and training of young people. The church was also the prime social organization that farm families attended. After church was over, there would be much visiting and talk about crops, the weather, and activities during the week. Usually, we children couldn't wait to get home, as Sunday afternoon was our "time off" and, in the summer months, we were anxious to start a ballgame or to go fishing. My father or mother never worked the fields on Sunday. Sunday was a day of rest, and either they would use Sunday afternoons for visiting family or church friends (which I remember that I didn't like very much), or they would just take a nap and rest from all of the week's physical work. But, come four-thirty in the afternoon, it was time for the evening chores to begin and all hands were expected to be there and ready to go to work.

The history of the Chippewa Church of the Brethren, as recounted by Donna Rehm, clearly shows that most of the jobs in the church were done by church members who volunteered, and they were not paid for their work—a very important distinction in understanding how our church functioned. The church's organization consisted of a group of people who gave of their own time to preserve the religious tradition of the church and to help spread the word of the gospel. There were no "janitors." The women and sometimes the men met on a weekday to clean the church. There were no hired organists or pianists or soloists to provide music on Sunday. On special occasions, the children in a particular Sunday school class provided music on a Sunday morning. All of these jobs were done by volunteers who loved music and loved to sing praises to the Lord.

The organizational structure of the church was rather simple, too. For all of my recollection, there was always a full time minister. I do remember the Rev. Paul Shrider, who was hired as a part-time minister in 1944, but only because he once returned to the farm for a visit. Besides having a full-time minister, there was a Women's Organization that tended to preparing meals for special occasions and funerals and, as I recall, they gathered to make quilts, which were given to those who were less fortunate. Conversely, there was a Men's Organization, which met to work on the church building or grounds or to do any other job that was deemed men's work.

According to Donna Rehm's account, every member was given a silver dollar in 1948. I would have been eight years old, and I remember that event. My father "invested" the money in a litter of pigs, which he was raising on the farm, and when it came time to return the money to the church, the original investment and some of the profit from the sale of the pigs were returned to the church. I remember this event, since my father said that I helped take care of the pigs. Then someone in the church said that the pigs I took care of "made real hogs out of themselves," and everyone laughed!

I received my first bible from my mother and father on Christmas 1948 when I was eight years old, and it is signed in my mother's hand. And I still have this bible although its leather cover is all worn and scuffed on the corners. I recount this story, but not because I want you to believe that I am some kind of a pious religious person. Far be it, as my bible has spent many more years laying on a shelf than being opened and read! No, I recount this story because of the investment that my parents made in me and their never-ending belief in the goodness of God and his loving kindness! And little by little, the contents of this book have slowly sunk into my head, just as a slow, steady summer rain soaks into the dry ground! It was I who chose the zippered leather cover because I knew that this book needed all of the protection it could get from a young child who liked to play ball more than to sit in a Sunday school class! But the pages inside are still in good shape and the teachings recorded there have guided me throughout my whole life.

My religious education continued during the summer months too. For several years, I attended the Oak Grove

Mennonite Church's summer vacation summer bible school. This church was located about ten miles east of our house. A neighbor lady, Mrs. Worth, would take her son Bob and me there and pick us up around noon for the two weeks that the bible school was in session. And it was during these summers that my bible had its greatest use and abuse as it would be left lying on the ground while we played ball or went for a walk in the woods. I remember that this school was taught mostly by young Mennonite girls and I was impressed as to how many bible verses these people could recite from memory. In fact, there would be contests each morning to see how many verses one could recite from the bible. It was there that I learned the shortest verse in the bible: "Jesus wept." And at the end of the two weeks, the students of the bible school would put on a program for the parents, singing songs and reciting verses that were learned in the school.

On the other hand, the road to public school literally began at church—Geyers Chapel Church. A one-acre part of the Bupp Farm had been deeded to the Geyers Chapel Church in the 1860's, and the church building stood at the corner of Geyers Chapel Road and Hutton Road. The cemetery stood to the west of the church and was bordered by the church building, itself, and an iron fence that ran along Hutton Road. There were three or four beautiful maple trees planted along the iron fence. The other two sides of the cemetery were bordered by hedge bushes and an electric fence, which kept our cows out of the cemetery! Geyers Chapel Church was located about a quarter of a mile down the road from the house where I grew up, and it was here that the school bus would stop to pick us up in the morning and drop us off in the afternoon. An attached covered entrance way stood in front of the church. The entrance way was open to the north, and my brother John and I used to stand in that area as we waited for the bus. It provided a shield from the bitter cold west wind.

I do remember attending the Geyers Chapel Church one Sunday when I was about six years old. It was a very snowy Sunday morning, and the roads were covered with deep snow, so I walked down the road by myself to attend Sunday School there. (This was the only time that I can remember that our family did not attend church together on Sunday morning.) The Geyers Chapel Church was a very small brick building, painted white on the outside. Sunday school classes were much like those of a one-room school house and were held over a big iron register in the floor, which was directly above the coal fired furnace in the basement of the church. The church did not have indoor toilets, but rather had two outhouses in the back. I can remember trying to read from the bible that Sunday morning and I was a bit ashamed as my reading skills were not very good at that point in my life. After I left the farm, the Geyers Chapel Church was torn down and the congregation moved into the old Smithville Methodist Church building in Smithville, Ohio, where my Grandfather and Grandmother Bupp had attended church. The Methodists built a new building across the street in Smithville. The Geyers Chapel Church's cemetery still remains on the corner of the farm.

The public school I first attended was Smithville Elementary School, and it was located about five miles from our home. But, because of the school bus route, the ride usually lasted about forty-five minutes either way, so it seemed that the little village of Smithville, Ohio, was located much farther away than it really was from the farm.

I can recall my first day at school. My brother John showed me the entrance to the first-grade school room and then disappeared! And so began my journey for the next seven years at the Smithville Elementary School building. My first-grade teacher was Mrs. Fitzpatrick, and she was regarded as a very good teacher. We had a cafeteria in the school and, as best as I can remember, first graders ate their lunch in the cafeteria, but all of the other grades had to take their trays to their home rooms, since the cafeteria was not big enough to accommodate everyone. There were two recesses during the day, one in the morning and one in the afternoon, and we children would go outside to play on the swings or to play ball. Recesses were staggered so that the playground wouldn't be overflowing with children.

The remarkable thing about my public school education was that most of the children who were my classmates in first grade also graduated with me from high school some twelve years later! There was stability to the families of the children that attended Smithville Schools that is missing in today's society. People who lived in this rural community lived there all of their lives. This made a huge difference as to how one interacted with class mates, with teachers, and with parents. Each grade had its own room, and you remained in that room until you graduated to the next grade. It wasn't until I attended eighth grade that several of the local schools were combined into Green Local School, and our class was joined by students from Madisonburg and Marshallville. Even so, there were only sixty-two in my graduating class at Smithville High School!

Your school mates were like family. So were the teachers, the school bus drivers, and all who worked in the school system. And to make matters even more tightly knit, my father served on the school board for many years. No one could get very far out of line in a system like that! In those days, teaching was a vocation and a way of life, not just another job. And the teachers that I had made huge sacrifices to their vocation as they truly loved what they did.

There was very little in the way of religious conflicts. In the school system that I attended, approximately sixty percent of the students were Mennonite. The Mennonite families were God fearing people who were predominately farmers. They drove cars and owned tractors with rubber tires and went to church each Sunday just like my family. I do remember that in grade school, we did have one hour of religious education a week during sixth and seventh grade. There were twin girls, Jean and Jane Gerig, who were Catholic by faith, and they would go to another room when we had our one hour of religious education. The Gerig girls were identical twins and they dressed exactly alike. Later in high school, I dated both of them briefly, and I was one of the few people in the class who could instantly tell them apart!

Music has always been a part of my life. I believe that it was during third grade that we had a little rhythm band in school. Our instruments were blocks of wood, some blocks being covered with sandpaper so that they would make a shuffling sound, and there was a triangle, a cymbal, and a drum. In fourth grade, we had a little band that actually had instruments, and that was when I started to play the trumpet. I used a hand-me-down trumpet from my brother John. The only time that I can remember taking any formal lessons was one summer when I was in the eighth grade. During eighth grade, I was a member of a little swing band. Ronnie Hartzler played the accordion, Karen Steuart played the clarinet, Janet Dilyard played the saxophone, and I played the trumpet. We used to practice together, and we won a school-sponsored talent contest that year. I remember playing my trumpet outside in the morning as I waited on the school bus, and the neighbors reported that they could hear me from several miles away!

Music was the one extracurricular activity that my parents fully supported, and I played my trumpet in the high school concert band and the marching band, which performed on various school occasions. On Memorial Day, the marching band would lead a parade from the high school to the Smithville cemetery. After a speech and gun salute from the veterans, the band would head back to the school. The marching band would perform at the high school football games, and we had a lot of fun riding on the band bus, singing, and playing at half time. Our little band marched five across and eleven deep! A very small band when compared to today's school bands. But the excitement of Friday night football games, the half-time performances, and the singing and whooping it up on the band bus are all things that I will never forget.

I had an interest in shortwave radio and amateur radio when I was in the eighth grade. I built a small radio transmitter, and my parents bought me a shortwave radio. I used to spend many nights listening to the hams on the radio or to radio stations located in Europe. One of my school teachers, Harold Taylor, used to work with a group of boys after school, trying to teach us Morse Code. Mr. Taylor had served time in the Navy, and he was just one of many examples of teachers who loved teaching and gave extra time to the job. He knew electronics and often said that he could make a lot more money working somewhere else, but teaching was his love. I became proficient enough in Morse Code to pass my novice license (KN8BWD) by borrowing some records and a record player from Glen Hartzler, who was a class mate. Another class mate, Ronnie Hartzler, also received his novice license and later passed the test for a technician class phone ham radio license. But my interest in amateur radio dwindled, and I never really got into this form of communication.

My high school years passed quickly. And it was a "transformation" time for me. My older brother John was the athlete in the family, and he played basketball throughout his high school years. I played basketball in my freshman year, but that effort was not particularly successful as my physical ability to play the sport was limited by my skill and by asthma—a condition that shuts off your breathing just when you need it most! But as someone once said, "If one door of opportunity closes, another door will surely open." And so I filled my spare time with other extra-curricular activities.

I spent four years in the band, four years in speech club, three years on the debate team (we managed a second in

Wayne County one year) , two years in the dance band, two years in the Junior and Senior class play, two years on the Mosaic staff, which was the high school newspaper, one year as the business manger of the Fabrica, which was the high school year book, one year in the Future Teachers Association, one year in radio club, one year in the chorus, one year in the boys' glee club, and one year playing basketball! Also for two years, I was elected into two honor organizations at Smithville High School: The National Honor Society and Quill and Scroll. And so it should become clear that I liked music and liked to have fun, but also, I began to learn how to compete with others by using my mind instead of my physical strength.

And there were so many teachers who helped guide us along the way. Teachers who unselfishly gave of themselves: Mr. Thornton McCay, who was the high school principal and ruled with a large wooden paddle (literally); our high school class advisor, Mr. Jack Dorricott, who was also was one of my debate coaches; two English teachers, Mrs. Alta Murray, who coached the Senior class play, and Mrs. Joan Ramseyer, who directed the Junior class play and was also one of my debate coaches; Mr. Lowell Frantz, who was the music teacher; and Mrs. Eileen Barrett, who taught journalism and ran her classes like those in college. She gave us the freedom to develop our writing, reporting, and business advertisement skills. Of course, there were many others, but these teachers in particular, along with Mr. Taylor, who headed the radio club, helped to mold and shape my life, and above all, taught me to have fun while doing it!

It was also during my high school years that our nation became interested in space exploration and space travel, and when I was a freshman in high school, a number of us—Glen Hartzler, Jim Hutchinson, and I—became interested in amateur rocketry. After doing very little experimentation, we built a sleek-looking rocket with the assistance from some of the teachers in school. The body of the rocket was made out of a two-foot piece of chrome-plated, brass drain pipe, which we bought at Jakey Worth's hardware store in Smithville. The industrial arts teacher, Mr. Dale Roe, turned the nose cone out of a piece of hard wood on one of the school lathes. He also turned the engine nozzle out of a piece of brass and cut the fins from some flat steel stock.. The formula for the fuel—zinc dust and sulfur—came from *Scientific American*. The launch of this rocket took place on Glen Hartzler's farm, which was located only about three or four miles away from the Bupp Farm. The event was witnessed by our science teacher, Mr. Taylor, and our home room teacher, Mr. Dorricott, who brought his high speed movie camera to photograph the event. Fortunately, we were smart enough to electrically launch the rocket, which turned out to be nothing more than a two and half pound bomb!

At any rate, the rocket was launched, and that was the last that any human being ever saw of that rocket! Years later when the high speed movies were reviewed at one of my class reunions, there were only four frames of pictures from that event: the rocket on the launch pad, flame shooting from the exhaust nozzle, a curious bulge forming just in front of the fins, and the last frame, which was entirely filled with a red ball of fire! We never did try to build another rocket or to do additional experimentation to determine what went wrong, and our school teachers wisely did not encourage any further investigations!

Subsequent to our failed rocket launching, probably the single most important historical event that happened during my high school years was the launching of the Soviet Sputnik satellite in 1957. I was a junior in high school at the time and this event was truly a direction-changing event for me in regards to what I wanted to do with my life. Before the launch of the Soviet satellite, educational achievements were sort of frowned upon by my peers and one was labeled a "brown noser" if you became too close to your teachers! But, with the launching of Sputnik, it suddenly became clear that we (The United States of America) were not the world leaders any more, and that our country had a lot of catching up to do. We first felt fear as Sputnik circled over our heads and its constant beeping kept us wondering what the Soviets were trying to do. Was this grapefruit sized satellite trying to spy on us? Would it fall out of the sky and land on us? No one knew the answer to these questions, but they clearly shook us out of a deep sleep. I didn't change over night. Neither did our schools change over night. But this one event clearly helped me set my sights on pursuing an education in science, and my career choice became not only acceptable, but deemed as necessary, by society. A whole new universe had just opened up to me, and I wanted to be a part of it!

CHAPTER 4
CELEBRATION OF HOLIDAYS AND MAJOR LIFE EVENTS

Much of our daily life on the farm was repetitive and seamless in nature. The morning and evening chores of feeding and watering the animals, gathering and packing the eggs, and milking the cows went on regardless of whether the day was a Sunday or a holiday. So it should come as no surprise that holidays were something in addition to the daily routine and chores and not something separate from the daily routine. Yes, we did celebrate holidays, but our celebrations were much different from how these same holidays and life events are celebrated today. Part of what is written here is a blend of family traditions and circumstance, but it also deeply reflects the close ties that the family had to the church and to the teachings of Jesus.

Christmas was a religious celebration. My mother did have a few decorations that she put up for Christmas, and the ones I remember were a set of electric candles that were placed in the dining room window, which could be seen from the road, and several paper bells that were hung in the various doorways in the house. My father would buy a small Christmas tree and then struggle with mounting the tree in a big block of salt that he used as the base. These blocks of salt were quite heavy and were placed on a metal stake that was driven into the ground in the pasture so that the cows would be able to get some salt during the day. At any rate, the block of salt made an acceptable Christmas tree stand as it had a hole formed in the center of the block, and he and brother John would fit the tree into the hole and then secure the tree with a couple of wooden wedges. That was pretty much the end of my father's Christmas duties and the decoration of the tree was up to my mother and us children.

My mother and my brothers helped decorate the tree. We did have a string of electric Christmas lights, some strings of silver garland, and a few boxes of lead tinsel. We would also make popcorn and string the kernels of popped corn on a long string and hang that on the tree for decoration. Some of the popped corn was also coated with melted sugar and made into popcorn balls, which were a real Christmas treat.

There were very few presents given at Christmas time. Of course, we children clamored for Christmas presents and I can recall my father saying that, "all I ever got for Christmas was an orange and some popcorn balls and I was happy with that!" My mother and father did not exchange Christmas gifts, nor did they buy or exchange gifts with their parents or with their brothers and sisters. However, we children did receive presents on Christmas morning, and there were two in particular that I recall to this day. When I was six years old, I received a Marx electric train set. I know exactly the year as my father wrote the year on the box with the words "guess who" next to the year 1946. This was no plastic train set. No, toys in those days were made out of metal and, to me, that train was very realistic in detail. The engine had a head light and pulled a coal tender, box car, gondola car, and a caboose. We would lay on the floor and turn off the lights in the dining room and watch the train going around and around on the tracks with its head light brightly shinning. It was something that I had truly wanted and I played with that train set for many years. Several accessories were later added: a piece of plywood for a roadbed, a metal trestle bridge, and a tower with two spot lights.

A few Christmases later, perhaps when I was eight or nine years old, I received a Daisy BB gun. Again, it was something that I had truly wanted and my parents gave in to my wishes. There was an endless supply of English sparrows on the farm and from that time on, none of them were safe! Over the years, I dispatched a lot of sparrows with that gun as well as quite a few tin cans! I learned how to handle and shoot a gun. We used to set a tin can on the old oil tank that stood in front of the smoke house and shoot at the tin can from the back porch. However, my father took a dim view of our using the side of the smoke house as a back stop when he saw all of the BBs stuck in the siding!

Christmas Day was always celebrated with a dinner, and I can remember going to my Grandmother Bupp's home one Christmas. As was her tradition, she made tripe, or cow's stomach, for Christmas dinner. The inside of the cow's stomach was filled with meat, vegetables, and potatoes, and the entire dish was then baked in the oven. I can remember my mother saying that it wasn't one of her favorites, but I ate it anyway and it tasted good to me! Grandmother and Grandfather Bupp also had an assortment of nuts during the holidays, and they had a wooden bowel that was turned out of a tree trunk. The bowel held the nuts and several small tools that were needed to crack the nuts. After dinner, we would sit in the living room and talk. During the course of the conversation, we would crack some of the nuts and eat them. Grandfather Bupp also made some simple wooden toys for my brother John for Christmas in his basement. One toy that I remember was a wooden cart that I used to play with.

My mother also made lots of delicious cookies for Christmas, and these cookies were the kind where you roll out the dough and cut out the cookies with a tin cookie cutter in the shape of a Christmas tree or a star or a snowman. We would help frost the cookies with brightly colored red, green, yellow, and white frosting and then sprinkle some brightly colored bits of sugar onto the cookies. The snowmen were decorated with red cinnamon candies as buttons. I particularly liked the snowman and thoroughly enjoyed biting off the head of the snow man and making him disappear!

The birth of the baby Jesus was celebrated at church on the Sunday nearest to Christmas Day. The children would usually sing Christmas songs, and then we received an orange and a small bag of candy from the Sunday school for our efforts.

Memorial Day was a day of remembrance for loved ones who had died. In fact, Memorial Day was called Decoration Day or Flag Day, and it was used as a day to visit the graves of my mother's mother or my father's father and to plant flowers on their graves. I can remember my mother visiting her mother's grave in the East Chippeaw Church's cemetery. There, she would plants geraniums on Decoration Day and spend time reflecting on her mother's life. In the meantime, I would play among the tombstones and wait till she had finished planting the flowers and paying her respects. It was a somber occasion and a sad time for my mother as I can remember her tears, although she never spoke of her mother after we left the cemetery.

Nothing was ever mentioned in our home about all of the war veterans who lost their lives fighting for this country. You see, the Church of the Brethren members are pacifists, and we did not believe in taking another person's life. There was never any mention in church of the people who lost their lives in past wars. Later, when I was in high school and in the marching band, we used to march from the high school to the Smithville Cemetery and, there, the veterans would hold a short ceremony that included a speech and a gun salute to those who had died fighting for our country. The individual graves of veterans were "decorated" by marking the grave with a small United States flag. I have always been in conflict with myself in regards to following the teachings of our church, which forbade taking another human life and serving in our armed forces. And, in particular, I thought that the church should recognize those who had fought and died for our country.

On the other hand, Thanksgiving was a very special and a joyful occasion. We understood the old hymns of Thanksgiving when we sang "Come, Ye Thankful People Come," or "We Gather Together" in a way much different from those folks who buy their food in a supermarket. I can still hear my mother singing, "Come, ye thankful people come, raise the song of harvest home; all is safely gathered in, ere the winter storms begin!" Yes, Thanksgiving was a special time for folks who had worked all summer long planting, cultivating, and harvesting. There was great satisfaction in knowing that the barn and the granary were full, that the animals would have enough to eat during the winter, and that they would be able to produce milk, which sustained our livelihood. Likewise, there was a great satisfaction and security in knowing that the fruit cellar cupboard was filled with canned fruits, vegetables, and meats and that there were squash, carrots, and Chinese cabbage stored in the root cellar for the winter months ahead.

My mother would prepare the traditional Thanksgiving turkey dinner. We all enjoyed turkey, but my father would say that leftover turkey gets old quick after the second day. My mother would start the day before Thanksgiving to prepare the dinner (which was served around one in the afternoon) by making pumpkin and apple pies for dessert. She would get up very early at 4:00 a.m. Thanksgiving morning to start the turkey in the oven. There would be dressing stuffed inside the turkey while it was baking and outside dressing that contained bits of turkey meat and then baked in a separate pan by itself.

The Thanksgiving meals that I remember best were attended by my Uncle Arnie, his wife Edna, and my cousin Leland. They would usually arrive just before dinner. While my mother was preparing the Thanksgiving dinner, we men would use the morning to clean out the straw sheds where the cows stayed during the day when they couldn't go out to pasture. I don't know what it was about Thanksgiving morning, but it always seemed that this was the ideal time to begin the yearly job of cleaning out the manure from the straw shed! One of the requirements for this job was that the fields had to be frozen so that the tractor and the manure spreader would not bog down in the field. Maybe it was my father's way of telling us to appreciate what we had and to be thankful for our dinner. I do not know. At any rate, we would gather at the table that my mother had prepared and enjoy the fruits of our labors! Even though Uncle Arnie was rather thin, he could certainly eat his share of food and frequently finished his Thanksgiving dinner with two pieces of pie—one apple and one pumpkin—when given the choice of which kind he would like! The tables were cleared and the dishes were washed by my aunt Edna and my mother.

Thanksgiving was about the only day (only the afternoon actually) that my father ever took off to go hunting. We would frequently go hunting in the afternoon with my Uncle and my father. We boys never carried guns. My father and my uncle were the bearers of the guns and it was our job to fan out on each side and try to kick up a rabbit or a cock pheasant. Usually the hunt was successful, and there would be one less rabbit on the farm.

The birth and death of animals were much a part of life on the farm. And so it was with the coming and passing of human life. But according to the teachings of the Church of the Brethren, a baby would not be baptized into the church until much later in the child's life. There was a ceremony that was called baby dedication, where the parents would bring the child forward and dedicate the life of the child to the church, but baptism into the church was reserved for much later in life when the child could understand the fundamental teachings of the church and was ready to accept those teachings as their personal beliefs. According to my Baptismal Certificate, I was baptized in 1950 when I was ten years old. Baptism followed the traditional teachings of the Bible, which were taught by John the Baptist and the event was celebrated by tri-immersion in a river! I do remember baptisms that occurred in the stream across the road from the church when the weather permitted, but for myself and most of those that followed after I joined church, there was a baptistery in the floor behind the pulpit. The baptistery was perhaps four feet deep and large enough for two people. It had to be filled with water, and I can remember helping my father fill the empty milk cans with water and load them onto the truck to take to the church. The preacher and the individual who was joining the church would walk down several small steps into the baptistery and the preacher would pronounce the name of the person to be baptized, and say, "I baptize thee in the name of the Father, the Son, and the Holy Ghost," and with each pronouncement, the person would be fully immersed into the water! Hence, baptism was by tri-immersion. It was an event that I will never forget. You were not saved until you were baptized and joined The Church of the Brethren.

It does seem a bit strange to me that birthdays were not celebrated in our family! I do not remember my mother or father ever exchanging birthday greetings or gifts! I didn't know my own mother's birth date until after I left the farm, Once, when I was in seventh grade, I did celebrate my birthday with a party at our home with several of my friends. But, in general, birthday presents were not given and family birthdays were just another day. I do not understand why birthdays were not celebrated in the family. Perhaps it was because my parents never permitted themselves the luxury of looking back or reflecting on milestones or other achievements that occurred in their lives. Their concept of time was always in the forward direction—tomorrow was just an extension of today with a short rest period in between, and the day after that would be just like tomorrow. I think that my mother truly believed in what she often said: "what is past is over and done with" and "don't cry over spilt milk!"

Death was an accepted end to life. I certainly understood about dead animals and disposed of quite a few of them during my time on the farm! We understood that animals did not have a soul and once they were dead, they were dead. Humans were different in that they possessed a soul and it was the human soul that departed from the dead body and went to be judged before God himself. But death was something that was not dwelt upon, and my parents remained focused on life and living life according to the teachings of the church. I still remember the words that we sang in church: "Work for the night is coming, work through the morning hours, work for the night is coming, when man works no more!" Yes, I realized that we were singing about the time when we would die, but the words of that great hymn kept our minds and energy focused on living this earthly life and not upon death. We did not worry about death as we trusted that the Lord would take care of us after we died.

I can remember when my Grandfather Bupp died in 1946. He had been ill and was in the hospital for some time. I can remember my sadness and the sadness of the family when he died, and the funeral that was held in the Smithville Methodist Church. As recounted by my Aunt Edna, he had suffered from severe pains in his chest and would often tightly bind a towel around his chest to help relieve the pain. After his death, an autopsy was not ordered by the family. As was the custom in those days, the body of my grandfather resided in my grandmother's home until the funeral. If there were visits by family or friends, it was done in the home and not at a funeral home.

The most sacred celebration of the Church of the Brethren was the Love Feast, or communion, as it is known today. The Love Feast was a reenactment of the Last Supper, which is well documented several places in the Bible. The one that was used in our ceremony is found in Luke, Chapter 22. Communion was held about four times a year in our church. Communion was a service separate from Sunday morning church, and only those folks who were members of the Church of the Brethren were invited to participate in the ceremony. This ceremony was held in the evening, and we would first gather in the sanctuary of the church. In a separate room, there would be two rows of tables set with a simple meal that consisted of ground beef, bread crumbs, and a pot of beef broth. Also on the table were some small pieces of unleavened bread, as the biblical communion is a celebration of the Passover, and small glasses of red grape juice, which were used in place of wine.

The occasion was very solemn in nature and the entire event was conducted by candle light. At the start of the Love Feast, the men and women would file into the banquet room and form two separate lines. The evening would start with a foot washing ceremony. This ceremony served to demonstrate humility and service to all people. All would remove their shoes and socks, and the first person in the row would put on an apron around his waist and then begin to wash the feet of the person next to him in a small basin of water, which contained a bar of soap. After washing and drying the feet with the towel, the two individuals would stand and exchange a kiss on the check in thankfulness of this lowly service before the apron was exchanged and the process would be repeated down the line. We boys did not line up with our fathers, and we would sometimes try to tickle the feet of one of our friends during the foot washing ceremony just to see if we could make them laugh! After everyone had their feet washed, the last person would return to the start of the line and wash the feet of the first person. One of the hymns that was sung during the foot washing ceremony was "My Jesus I Love Thee."

After the foot washing ceremony was complete, the celebration of the Passover meal as recounted in Luke came next. The Passover meal was known as the Last Supper, since it was the last meal the disciples had with Jesus before he was crucified. The dinner, which was prepared by the women of the church, would be eaten in silence. The only sounds heard would be the clinking of the metal spoons on the china dishes. After everyone had finished eating, communion was then taken by all. The small pieces of unleavened bread would be broken with the person who sat across the table, and then the glass of wine (grape juice) was drunk as prescribed in Luke. Everyone departed from this service in a very quiet and reverent mood.

Marriage was a deeply religious ceremony that was performed by the church. The teachings of Jesus in regards to marriage can be found in St. Matthew, Chapter 10, and strictly forbids divorce except in the case of unfaithfulness or death. There were no divorces in our family, and once you took the vows of marriage, it was a lifetime commitment. As I have written earlier, my Grandfather Yoder did remarry after his first wife died. I remember him saying, "it (life) just didn't go as well after my first wife died!"

I do remember the marriage of my brother John to Marilyn Joan Carmony in 1957. They were married on July 28th at the Evangelical United Brethren Church in

Madisonburg, Ohio, where she went. I do not remember much about the reception after the ceremony. Later in the year, on December 2, 1957, my brother joined the army and left the country for a tour of duty in Germany in April of the following year.

One curious celebration of marriage that was sanctioned by the church and conducted in those times was called a "belling." Sometime after the young couple had wed, friends and neighbors would gather together late at night under the window of the newlyweds' bedroom and start to make a lot of racket by ringing bells and pounding on anything that would make noise so as to wake up the couple (and to interrupt anything else that might have been going on). Our Youth group did go to my brother John's home, which was then located across the street from the Wooster hospital and we did "bell" them! Jack Rehm, who was our Youth Leader, brought an old buzz saw blade and pounded on it with a hammer! I often wondered what the neighbors thought of that custom. Fortunately, either no one called the Police or we left before they arrived!

CHAPTER 5

RAISING FOOD FOR THE FAMILY

As was the custom on the farm, my mother raised the vegetables and preserved the food for the family. This in itself would be considered a full time job today. And it was from my mother's teaching that I learned how to tend a garden. We had a garden behind the house, perhaps seventy-five feet by one-hundred feet, that was devoted solely to raising the vegetables consumed by the family. "Organically grown" wasn't something that was just invented yesterday; it was how our vegetables were grown in the garden on the farm! My mother's garden consisted of two huge raised beds perhaps about twenty-five feet across. The two beds were separated by a walkway or path that was lower than the beds, and there were also paths on the outside of the two beds. On the outer sides of the garden, there were two narrower raised beds, perhaps three feet deep that ran along the length of the garden. The entire garden was surrounded by a fence, and there was an iron gate at the end nearest to the house. The fence and the gate were necessary to keep out the chickens and the rabbits! As one entered the garden through the gate, the first fifteen feet of the garden area was part of the lawn. Some grape vines ran along the fence nearest to the house, as well as a couple of raspberry bushes.

It was on this plot of land that my mother toiled from early spring till late fall, growing all of the fresh vegetables that we enjoyed during the summer growing season. The land was tilled entirely by my mother as she spaded it by hand with a shovel, hoeing the freshly spaded ground, and then raking it smooth in preparation for the planting of seeds. Sometimes my brother and I would help with spading the garden, and it was always our job to bring loads of rotted cow manure in the wheel barrow, which gave sustenance to my mother's garden. A pile of cow manure was started outside of the barn in the fall. This pile was a mixture of cow manure taken out of the barn after milking time and wheat straw, which was used as bedding for the cows. It would rot down (compost) during the winter months and made an excellent organic fertilizer. My mother would spade two rows across her garden, turning over the soil to bury any small weeds and their seeds. Then the cow manure was placed into the trench left by the shovel. Again, two more rows were spaded across the garden, and the freshly turned earth would completely cover the rotted cow manure. This process was repeated again and again until a six- to ten-foot section of the garden was turned over. After turning over the ground, the clumps of earth had to be broken up with a hoe or smashed with the back side of the shovel and then smoothed with a rake until it was ready for planting the seeds or vegetable plants. The entire garden was not prepared all at once, but just enough to plant one or two types of vegetables that were ready to be planted.

The very first vegetables that my mother planted in the spring were left-over dried onions from the previous fall, which had begun to sprout in the cellar, and leaf lettuce seeds. The lettuce seeds were sown in one of the side beds. My mother would cover the seeds with an old burlap bag and carefully wet the burlap with water so that the seeds would quickly germinate. As soon as the first seeds began to sprout, the bag was removed. In the cool days of spring, the lettuce grew quickly and, when it was about three inches high, she would cut a small section that yielded just enough lettuce for dinner or supper, much like cutting the lawn grass. In a few days, the lettuce that had been cut would start to grow again, and there would be more lettuce for future cuttings. She made a wonderful dressing with fresh cream, a little sugar, and vinegar. And to my way of thinking, there is nothing better than leaf lettuce. The old dried onions that had begun to rot and sprout were also stuck into the ground. There, they began a new life and started to grow once more. Each eye of the onion gave birth to a new onion and, after they had grown to about 12 inches high, we ate them, either green or cut up into small pieces for the salad. Today, we call them scallions. I like them best when eaten raw.

Spring salads were something that I always looked forward to and while, today, we toil endlessly to kill the dandelions that grow in our manicured lawns, when I was growing up we ate the dandelions as an early spring salad—very tasty and very rich in iron! But, if you want to try a dandelion salad, you must cut the plant from the root at ground level before the plant blossoms, and then soak the leafy parts in water overnight to remove the bitterness. My mother made a kind of "gravy" for the salad that consisted of slices of hard boiled eggs, bits of bacon, and some cream, sugar, and a little vinegar. I truly did enjoy eating dandelions this way and, besides, they were free for the taking!

On the opposite side of the garden was a bed of rhubarb that came up each year since it is an annual plant. My father did enjoy his rhubarb pie, but I never did care for the taste. I think it's better if you add some strawberries with the rhubarb. Another spring treat that my father enjoyed was asparagus. It grew along the fence by the road and came up each spring. It was one of those vegetables that I somehow never would eat when I was growing up, but I have since learned that asparagus is a premium vegetable that is often served at the best dining establishments! To me, it was some kind of weed that came up each spring. In late spring it grew so tall that it had to be cut down, as it would reach the electric fence and short it out! Asparagus is cut when the shoots grow to about eight to twelve inches high. However, some of the spears must be left to grow during the summer so that the plant can renew its strength for the following season.

My mother raised all kinds of vegetables, and I ate most all of them. But my favorites were raw carrots, red beets, raw kohlrabies and Chinese cabbage. The part of my mother's garden that made the greatest impression on me was the tomato section. My mother followed her father's teachings and planted two rows of tomatoes about two and a half feet apart in one of the garden beds. The tomato poles were saplings cut in my grandfather's woods. After the tomato plants started to grow to about a foot high, an iron stake was driven into the ground by each of the tomato plants and a pole was inserted into the hole. A group of four tomato poles were tied together at the top to form a "wigwam" type of structure that served as a trellis that would hold up the tomato plants as they grew and kept them off the ground. Raising tomatoes started in March since my mother would raise her own plants from seed. She used the ground from the garden and sterilized it by baking it in the oven! (Don't try to raise tomatoes without using sterilized ground or sterilized potting soil as the young tomato plants will develop a mold and disappear overnight!) The tomato plants were then transplanted into small pots and set out in the garden after the final frost. It was either my brother's or my job to haul a few more wheelbarrows of rotted cow manure to the garden, and the entire area around the tomato plants was covered with about six inches of rotted cow manure. And did those tomato plants like the menu! At the end of the summer, we had lovely, red, ripe tomatoes for dinner each night, served with a little sugar on the slices. My mother would also can tomatoes for use during the long winter months.

My mother's vegetable garden was not only for raising vegetables; she would plant flowers at the end of the garden where you first entered into the garden. Her garden was not only a source of food and sustenance for the family but was also a thing of visual beauty. One of her favorite flowers in the garden was gladiolus, which bloomed later in the summer. During the summer months, she would spend many hours during the cool of the morning and then in the cool of the evening after supper, working in her garden and tending to her plants and flowers. She also raised geraniums in boxes on the front porch and in several flower beds, which were scattered around the lawn. I have retained my mother's love of gardening and her love of flowers, and I enjoy working in the soil and watching things grow. It is a partnership that I find very satisfying, and I know that she is watching to see if I am growing any geraniums.

The vegetable garden behind the house was not our only source of vegetables—far from it! Up the lane and behind the barn was an old apple orchard. My father never did take good care of the apple trees, but there were always plenty of apples in the fall to make cider vinegar or to make pie. Just beyond the apple orchard was a piece of ground we called the "truck patch." It was large enough to plow with a horse or, later on, with the tractor. In was in this plot of ground where my parents planted sweet corn, green beans, sweet potatoes, and strawberries. My father would tend to the strawberries, since they had to be transplanted every other year and covered with straw during the winter time. However, it was my mother who picked all of those delicious strawberries, and either canned or froze enough quarts to keep the family well supplied with strawberries during the winter months. I can recall one year when my mother picked and either froze or canned over 500 quarts of strawberries! The truck patch was cultivated with a one-horse drawn cultivator, or after my father sold his team of horses in 1946, the patch was cultivated with a garden tractor. Weeding around the plants was carefully done with a hoe by hand. I can remember the team of horses that my father kept in the barn; their names were Prince and Dick. And I also remember the day when I was six years old when a man came to the farm and drove away my father's team of horses. I remember it well because it was one of the few times that my father ever showed any emotion, and it was a sad day for him as he watched his team of horses being driven away. I do not know how long he had owned this team of horses, but even at an early age, I could sense the feelings that he had for his horses, as they had been his faithful workers for a long time. By this time, we already had two tractors, and the days of farming with horses were rapidly coming to an end. My father and also one of the neighbors used their horses to pull the wagons in the fields when there were sheaves of wheat or shocks of corn to be picked up. A team of horses works very well for those tasks that are "stop and go," since the horses would pull the wagon ahead and then stop on voice command. Try that with a tractor!

It always amazed me as to how much food my mother raised. And the vegetables that she raised were not only for the family, but were shared with neighbors and friends. I used to think that we supplied half of the folks who went to our church with fresh vegetables! But raising vegetables was a great source of pride and joy for my mother, and she willingly shared her bounteous harvest with all of her friends and relatives. My mother had a favorite hoe that she used in the garden and in the truck patch. The steel in the blade part of this hoe was worn paper thin and only a very narrow two and a half inches of the blade remained! I recount this story as she had literally worn out that hoe by using it to prepare the ground and to hoe out the weeds so she could raise vegetables for her family. It was her favorite tool, and it suited her purpose well. I have since thought about that hoe many times, and I guess that one could even think of having to work so hard as some kind of cruel and unusual punishment, but to my mother, her garden was a place of joy, and she labored there out of love for her family. And next to her kitchen, she was happiest when she was working in her garden.

My mother took care of the house, raised us boys, washed and mended our clothes, picked up our clothes after we had taken them off, and grew all of the vegetables for the family herself. In short, she was a homemaker, a profession that is looked down upon today and almost forgotten. But she was an equal economic partner with my father as they shared the work of the family farm. Besides being active in the church, my mother was a charter member in the Smithville Helping Hands Homemaker's Club, which was comprised of various local farm women in the area, and she remained a member there all of her life for more than sixty years. When I was quite young, my mother used to take me to the meetings, which were held in one of the members' homes, and I can remember having my first taste of coffee at one of those meetings. Since my mother always drank her coffee black, I too still prefer mine the same way!

My mother was a very hard working but caring person. One summer while I was in high school, she helped take care of Verdie Rennecker, who was a lady that was quite old and in failing health. She lived in a small house at the end of the lane where her brother, Quinter Rennecker, lived. I would drive my mother there to Verdie's small home, and my mother would take a couple of quarts of canned beef and beef broth with her and see to it that Verdie had food and to help her get out of her chair and encourage her to walk a little each day if only to check for the mail in the mail box. I wondered why my mother was paying so much attention to this old woman, so one day I asked her. She said that Verdie Rennecker had taken care of her mother when she was ill and dying, and then I understood. She was paying back an old debt.

CHAPTER 6

SUMMER WORK ON THE FARM

It was by no coincidence that schools in rural communities let out for the summer by the middle of May. This might seem a little strange to you now but remember that the really hard work of planting and harvesting field crops grown on a farm begins as soon as the soil can be worked in early May. Today, schools run until the middle or end of June. Summer vacation is really a vacation time for today's children (what are we going to do now mom?), but not so for members of a family farm. For us rural folks, it was time for the men to begin the really serious work in the fields, which would sustain the animals and the family during the long winter days and nights.

Being successful as a farmer greatly depends not only upon the weather but also on the timing of when the seeds are planted, when the hay is cut to dry, or when the wheat is ready to be combined. And so it should come as no surprise that my father constantly listened to the radio. He would get up in the morning at 4:00 a.m. and go to the basement to clean and pack the eggs. And while he was working there, he would listen to the latest weather forecast on a small radio that he had there. When we milked cows in the barn, the radio in the barn was constantly on, not for our enjoyment of the latest popular songs that were being played, but mostly he would listen to the latest weather forecast, which would help him make the final decision on what had to be done in the fields that day. I remember one radio program that came on in the morning and evening at six, called the "Gold Star Report," which began with chickens cackling and marching band music! They advertised Gold Star Feeds, which were sold in nearby Wooster, Ohio, but more importantly, the program gave the latest weather forecast as well as prices of farm commodities of essential interest to my father. Even before and after meals, the radio in the house would be tuned to the news, and woe to anyone in the house who made noise or caused any disruption during the time that the weather forecast was being broadcast!

The first crop to be planted in early spring was corn. As I explained earlier, my father did all of the plowing himself. The ground was then disked to break up the chunks of fresh earth. Prior to planting, the ground was again worked with a spring harrow and a cultipacker, which was pulled behind the harrow. My father was very set in the ways that he worked the land and planted his fields. The corn was planted using the "checked" method of planting corn as opposed to drilling the corn. With the checked method, corn is planted in hills spaced evenly apart. One has to unroll a special spool of wire from one end of the field to the other. This spool of wire had "knots" in the wire about every 30 inches. The corn planter planted two rows of corn at a time. There were two circular "bins" on either side of the corn planter, which fed kernels of corn and fertilizer to the rows that were being planted. The wire was first stretched and staked at either end of the field. The tractor and the corn planter were then aligned with the stretched wire and the wire was attached to the trip mechanism that would cause the planter to drop some corn and fertilizer whenever one of the wire knots passed through the trip mechanism. This method of planting corn was essentially a mechanical way of planting the corn in hills. About three or four kernels of corn were dropped into each hill. When I think about it, this was perhaps a throw back to hand planting corn in hills, but my father claimed that it would give him more yield per acre than the other method of drilling the corn where the planter continuously released the corn along the row. The rate of release could be controlled, but if one planted the corn kernels too closely, the plants would be stunted. Likewise, if the corn kernels were spread too far apart, there would be wasted space between the plants. At any rate, checking the corn was the method that my father preferred and that was his method. And he loved straight rows. He would walk the wire before starting to plant the corn and pick it up and lift it high over his head, and then return it to the ground. This he did for the length of the field. Perhaps it was the straightness of this wire that made him want to plow his fields in a perfectly straight line. I do not know. An arm with a metal "spike" at the end of the arm was located on the side of the corn planter opposite to the checking wire. When this arm was extended, it made a line in the soil so one could position the planter on the return trip. After making one complete round, the wire then had to be moved over so that another four rows could be planted. I never did measure up to my father's standard of plowing or making rows straight enough when working the fields, but even today I use the "boot" method of fertilizing my lawn with my drop spreader. I take an old pair of boots, and use one to mark where I started the round and then, at the other end, I place the second boot to mark where the spreader wheel should end on the return trip. My neighbors think I am nuts, but I am only following the methods I learned from my father when I was growing up on the family farm!

Corn in those days was cultivated (as opposed to spraying herbicides on the corn to prevent weeds), and the tractor's rear wheels had to be adjusted so that they wouldn't smash down the rows of corn. The front tires on our tractors were already set together. The cultivators were attached to the front of the tractor and also to the rear of the tractor. Four rows of corn were cultivated in a single pass, and the cultivators were lifted up mechanically when one came to the end of the field. The corn required cultivation for the first time when it was perhaps two or three inches high. Timing of the first cultivation was important, since it was necessary to remove the weeds before they got a good start. The corn had to be cultivated perhaps two or three times until it become so tall that it would touch the tractor axle; by that time, the growing corn had won out over the weeds and would choke out any further weed growth. It was always my father's objective to have his corn "knee high by the fourth of July," because corn that passed this test was surely on its way to be ready to be picked in early fall, long before the snow arrived.

My father spent a lot of time observing and comparing his corn fields to those of the neighbors. My brother John and I would have to hand weed the ends of the field and also the rows along the road, so when one drove by our fields, not a weed could be spotted from the road! A beautiful corn field with perfectly straight rows and tall plants of corn all the same height brought much pleasure to my father. It was a sure sign that the crop would be good.

Perhaps the hardest work on the farm came in June when it was time to make hay, which usually began during the first week of June. It was the first cutting of hay that would be stored in the barn so that the cows would have hay for the winter. And since our farm was primarily a dairy farm, it was important that the cows had the best hay so they would continue to produce milk during the winter. As with most outdoor tasks on a farm, the weather played a key role in making hay. The hay would be cut with a cycle bar mower and then left laying on the field for one to three days until it became dry enough to bale. It was important that the hay did not receive any rain on it after it was cut, or it would soon lose most of its nutrients and begin to rot. And so began the guessing game that my father engaged in to determine when he should cut enough hay, which would dry and be ready for bailing before the next rain. After the hay was dry enough, it would be raked into windrows, and then the process of bailing the hay would began. My younger brother Sylvan frequently drove the tractor. My father would stack the bales onto the wagon, which was pulled behind the baler, and my older brother John and I would unload the wagons and stack the bales in the barns. It was always a race to see if we could keep up with the bailer in the field. Our wagons held eighty-three bails of hay, each weighing perhaps seventy-five to eighty-five pounds. I can remember one particularly hot summer day when we made fifteen loads of hay in a single day! Needless to say, we were exhausted for about two days after that, but there is something to the old saying of "making hay while the sun shines," and my father certainly subscribed to that saying! We did not work the fields on Sunday, although the cows still had to be milked, the eggs collected, and the animals fed. Making hay was a dusty, hot, back-breaking job, but it was the first harvest job of the summer. After the first cutting of the hay was made, the grass was allowed to grow again and, during August, a second cutting of hay was often made. The second cutting contained more clover and alfalfa grasses, which were very rich in nutrients and this hay was usually fed to the calves or young cattle.

Beginning around the first part of July, the wheat would be ready to be combined. Wheat was a crop that was planted late in the fall in the same field where corn had grown over the summer. The ground would first be prepared for planting the wheat, and then the wheat was sown in the newly prepared field. The wheat would sprout and begin to grow when the fall rains came and would survive the winter and begin to grow again in the spring, shooting up to about two and half feet tall. The tassels that contain the kernels of wheat appeared after the wheat had grown several feet high. Wheat was a prized crop by farmers, not only for income from the sale of the wheat, but also for the straw left behind on the field after the wheat was separated from the stalks. After combining the wheat, the wheat stubble was cut closely to the ground, and then windrowed and bailed into bales. The bales of straw were stored in the barns and used for bedding for the cattle during the winter months when the cows couldn't go out to pasture. Wheat straw also makes a good mulch for the garden and, when plowed or mixed into the soil, it helps to keep the soil loose. The Case combine that my father owned would cut a swath of wheat perhaps six or seven feet wide in one pass, cutting off the stalks about six inches from the ground. The combine separated the wheat kernels from the straw and the chaff and stored the wheat in a bin on the combine. My brother John and I would fill up the old 1947 Dodge pickup with wheat and then drive the truck to the granary in the barns where the wheat had to be hand shoveled off the truck and then hand shoveled into the grain bins. Another back breaking job! It was by no accident that I learned to drive the truck on the farm long before I was old enough to drive on the roads! I can remember on one occasion when brother John got too close to the combine and put a deep gash into the cab of the truck, which remained there for as long as we owned that truck. We worked as fast as we could to unload the wheat and return to the field so that my father could empty the bin on the combine and keep the machine going. It was not uncommon to find us still combining late into the evening after the cows had been milked. The wheat has to have a certain moisture content (less than 16%) before it can be safely stored in the granary. If the moisture content is too high, the wheat will spoil or mold. So, when a bright sunny day came along, and the wheat's moisture content tested

OK, we only stopped long enough to milk the cows in the evening, and then it was out to the fields again to keep on combining.

Bailing straw (whether it be wheat or oat straw) didn't seem as hard, since the bales were lighter, perhaps sixty to sixty-five pounds each. Also, the acreage of wheat that could be planted and sold for a guaranteed price was limited by the government. As I recall, my father was limited to about fifteen or twenty acres of wheat, which in acreage was about one-third of the amount of hay that we raised. My father also raised about fifteen acres of oats, and the straw from the oats was also used for animal bedding, and that helped to make up for the limited amount of wheat that could be raised.

One of the last outside jobs of the summer was to fill the silo with chopped corn. This would usually occur around Labor Day, as the corn needed to mature enough so that the kernels on the ears had already dented, and the leaves on the stalks started to show some brown. The three staples that kept the milk cows in production during the winter months were "ensilage" or chopped corn, hay, and "chop," which was a mixture of ground up grains—corn, wheat, and oats. My father strongly believed that the chopped corn was essential so that the cows would have enough bulk in their diets. He did not like grass silage, as he believed that it did not contain enough bulk for the cows' digestive system.

Today, one machine cuts off the stalks of corn and chops the stalks and then blows the chopped corn into a wagon. But that was not the way it was done some fifty years ago. We had a corn binder, which was pulled behind the tractor. It took one row at a time, and then, when enough corn was cut to make a bundle, the machine would automatically tie a string around the bundle of stalks and drop it onto the ground. After the corn was cut with the binder, the corn chopper was set up near the base of the silo. One of the tractors was used to run the corn chopper with a long wide belt. The corn chopper contained three very sharp knives that cut the stalks of corn into small pieces, and then the machine blew the chopped pieces of corn up the pipe and over the top of the silo some forty to fifty feet above. The corn chopper we had was jointly owned by three or four neighbors, and when it was time to fill silos, the neighbors would bring their wagons and tractors and help gather up all of the bundles of corn that had been cut. One silo could usually be filled in one or two days. The woman of the house made dinner for all of the neighboring men who helped to fill the silo. I can remember the tables that were set out in the yard for the food, and the wash tubs of water, bars of soap, and clean towels so that the men could wash up for dinner. And what a feast we had as all were hot and hungry and much food was consumed. Silo filling was the one summer harvest task that was shared by the neighbors, but even this harvest chore eventually gave way to more modern equipment, which cut and chopped the corn or grass in one pass in the field.

School usually started right after Labor Day, but after one week, school was interrupted with the County Fair at Wooster. This was always a time that we looked forward to as they closed the County Schools for one day on Tuesday so that everyone could go to the fair. When I was growing up, it was the midway rides that were the big attraction as I had already seen enough cows, chickens, and horses in my lifetime! But the excitement of the midway rides, the call of the barkers to try to win a stuffed animal or a ribbon or to knock down some milk bottles was what caught my attention. The Wayne County Fair lasted one week, and it was a time for country folks to talk to each other, look at all of the produce and 4H projects, and to celebrate the end of the summer. It was also a time for the farmers to come and see all of the new farm equipment and maybe to dream about a new red tractor or a new wagon. We never exhibited any animals at the fair, as my father was always concerned about some disease that his cows might pick up there.

In late fall, it was time to pick the corn. My father owned a corn picker, which cut two rows of corn at a time and snapped off the ears of corn and removed the husks from the ears. The ears of corn were deposited in the wagon, which was pulled behind the corn picker. The ears of corn were then shoveled into a wire corn crib, which allowed the ears to further dry out. Most of the back-breaking work of shoveling the corn off the wagon was replaced when my father bought a gravity box grain wagon and we used an electric elevator to take the corn from the wagon and deposit it into the cribs. The dried corn was used as cow, hog, and chicken feed during the winter months.

My father was very particular about the way he farmed his land and the procedures he used. His farming techniques were learned from his father and from trial and error as he engaged in farming the land. He did much reading on the subject—i.e., *The Farm Journal* magazine—and spent a lot of time comparing his fields to the fields of the surrounding farms. My father never went on vacations and, other than going to church, he took no time for himself. Thanksgiving Day was an exception in that he and perhaps my Uncle Arnie would go hunting for a rabbit or a pheasant in the afternoon. My father owned only one gun—a double barrel 16-gauge shotgun, which he fired at most twice a year. He would usually miss the rabbit with the first barrel but would always connect with the second barrel. The only other time I can remember my father taking time off to hunt was in the fall when he would go into Mrs. Yates's woods and shoot a couple of squirrels. Squirrel tails usually adorned the outside of our smokehouse, signaling a successful hunting trip.

I can remember my father saying that "there are many men who can load corn bundles onto the wagon faster than I, but very few of them will still be in the field with me at the end of the day!" And that was the way he lived his life—he paced himself so that he could work the long hours and still get enough rest at night so that he could begin all over again at four the next morning!

CHAPTER 7

THE AUGUST VISITS FROM AUNTS, UNCLES, AND COUSINS

The hard work of the summer harvest was always broken up by visits from aunts, uncles, and cousins in August. It was a wonderful time for memorable family meals, playing with all of my cousins, and learning about family life different from that of the family farm.

My mother's brother, Truman Yoder, and his first wife Patsy would come and stay with us. They lived in Ft. Wayne, Indiana, and I can remember on one occasion, they came by train to Wooster, Ohio, and then hitch hiked out to the farm. They had six children: Vincent, Dennis, David, Larry, Sue Ann, and Connie. For sleeping, mattresses were placed on the floor and perhaps four or five slept on a mattress. We didn't mind giving up our bed as it was fun to have all of the cousins for a visit. My uncle Truman worked at International Harvester in

Ft. Wayne, Indiana, and in those days, vacations were taken all at one time, usually in the summer. My mother would spend most of the time in her kitchen, making some of the most wonderful meals you could imagine. She loved to cook for her brother and his family, and she was happy in her kitchen, serving breakfast, dinner, and supper to everyone for several weeks. She did this without help from any of the men, although Aunt Patsy would help with the dishes or if Grandfather Fred and Grandmother Rena came over for a visit, Grandmother Rena would help with the dishes too. There were times when she would serve Sunday dinners, and the men would go off to visit or to take a snooze, but as soon as the dinner dishes were done, she would start cooking again for supper, which was served a little later in the evening than usual. My mother was very proud of the food she raised and the meals she served. And she loved to be in her kitchen; cooking was one of those chores that she did with great love and pride. For this, she will always be remembered.

A favorite summer tradition of the Yoder Family was the turtle soup dinner. My Grandfather Fred Yoder used to tell how he hunted turtles—by feeling his way underneath overhangs and under rocks along the streams until he could feel the turtle, and then he would grab it and toss it onto the bank! But, for my brother John and I, we would set fishing lines in the stream. The lines had a rather large fish hook on the end, and a piece of raw chicken meat was attached to the hook as bate. The line was then cast out into the stream, and the loose end tied to a tree or large weed along the bank. We would check the lines once in the morning and once in the evening before dark. The turtles we caught were snapping turtles, which weighted about five pounds. They would swallow the bait, hook, and all! After pulling the turtle out of the water, we would cut the line a safe distance away from the turtle and then put the turtle into a large feed sack. My father would fill a fifty-gallon wooden barrel with water, and when we had caught perhaps a half dozen turtles, he would butcher them. The turtles were killed by holding a large iron bolt out to the turtle, and when Mr. Turtle grabbed onto the bolt, one stretched the head and neck back over the shell, and then cut off the turtles head with a butcher knife! Snapping turtles have one large tooth in the front of their mouths, and they are to be respected. Once they grab onto something, they clamp down firmly and do not let go! My mother would cook the meat of the turtles and make a soup that was prized by the Yoder family. The meat was mild—a little like chicken—but I never did develop a taste for it.

Summer was also the time when my Uncle Reno Bupp, his wife Ruth, and my cousins Sue Ann and Bonnie who lived in Tallahassee, Florida, would also come for a visit in August. Uncle Reno worked at Florida State University in Tallahassee as head of the Social Sciences Division in the library. They would come and stay at Grandmother Bupp's home across the road. I remember Reno as he helped Grandmother take care of her garden or rose bushes when he was there for a visit, but he wisely shunned helping with the hay making or lifting the bales in the barns! Cousin Bonnie liked the cows on the farm, and she would get up early in the morning to watch my brother John feed and water the heifers, which were kept in Grandmother Bupp's barn. She even thought the cows had such beautiful eyes—a thought that never entered my mind, since we lived on a dairy farm and most of the attention that was given to the cows was on the other end!

In the evenings, my brother John and I would often go over to Grandmother's house after chores were done and after we had had our supper. We would play Carrom, a game that is played with wooden rings and uses one ring as the shooter. The object of the game is to knock the wooden rings into pockets located in the corners of the board. Or we might watch TV. I would play hide and seek with my cousins at Grandmother's house, which had a pantry just off of the kitchen where we would hide. And then we discovered that there was a narrow stairs off of the pantry that led to the upstairs. It was great fun going into the pantry and then sneaking quietly upstairs to hide there! My uncle Reno died in January of 1972, right after his 62nd birthday. Aunt Ruth still lives in Tallahassee and celebrated her 100th birthday in October 2007. Aunt Ruth has been blessed with excellent health and always makes it a point to tell me that the State of Florida never did surrender to the Union Forces during the Civil War, since the war officially ended before the documents could be signed in Florida!

Grandmother Bupp had one daughter, Edna (Bupp) Carlson. She and her husband Arnold and my cousin

Leland would often come for a visit. They too would stay at Grandmother Bupp's house. My uncle Arnie was a school teacher in Polk, Ohio, then they moved to Ashland, Ohio, and finally to Westerville, Ohio, where Uncle Arnie became the Assistant Superintendent of the Westerville schools. Uncle Arnie just didn't quite fit into the Bupp mold, as he was soft spoken and had a great sense of humor. I shall always remember the example that he set, and I give him much credit for opening my eyes to the world of education, even though I never became a school teacher.

When all of the cousins would come for a visit, one of our favorite places of escape was to the springs at Mrs. Yates's Farm, which was located just east of our farm. We would go there for a cool drink of spring water that flowed from a two-inch pipe the year around. It was a wonderful respite from the summer heat, and we would take refuge from the heat of the sun under the many willow trees that were planted on her farm and on our farm along the banks of the small stream that flowed here. Those springs were an excellent source of water for the small stream, thereby providing several small "holes" or pools of water under the willow trees that would sustain blue gills or other small fish. And to go fishing was a real treat and break from all of the farm work.

It was not uncommon for early farms to have a spring for the purpose of cooling the milk from the cows as well as a source of water for the animals. And the Yates's Farm was blessed with two springs—one in the milk house beside the barn, and the other behind the house. The spring in the milk house was very close to Geyers Chapel Road. The spring water flowed into a concrete tank that was partially buried in the ground, and then the cans of milk would be lowered into the tank to be cooled before the milkman arrived. The water would flow out of the concrete tank and into the small stream across the road. Mother Nature's refrigeration!

There was also a spring in the back of the house. It flowed into a rather large pond that had been scooped out of the ground. The pond provided us with recreation in the winter months, as it would hold just enough water so that we could go ice skating there. We would shovel off the snow and then find some broken tree branches for "hockey sticks" and a small piece of wood for a puck, and the game was on! Most of us didn't have skates; we just played in our shoes! The pond eventually became filled with weeds, as the muskrats tunneled through the banks, thereby draining the pond. But we had great fun there when we were growing up.

Mrs. Yates was a very jolly woman, but when I think back on her life, she had a very tough life. I do remember her husband Bert Yates, who was a small man and not well. He passed away when I was growing up. I also remember that his body was in their home and that we boys went to visit her and pay our last respects to her deceased husband after he died, but we excused ourselves from the funeral that afternoon as we wanted to play ball! She seemed to understand. Mrs. Yates was left with all of the farming, and my father paid her a great compliment when he said, "that woman can ride a tractor as good as any man!" She did all of the field work by herself, but eventually, she rented out the farm to one of her neighbors. Mrs. Yates was a good friend of my Grandmother Bupp, and since Grandmother Bupp could not drive a car, she took my Grandmother Bupp to church every Sunday to the Smithville Methodist Church.

We usually asked permission to come onto Mrs. Yates's land and she would always willingly comply. Her spring at the barn gave respite from thirst and heat to many who traveled along Geyers Chapel Road and she willingly shared its cooling waters. We did not recognize at the time that water would someday become a valuable commodity, to be bought and sold just like a gallon of milk, only worth a lot more money than milk! And Mrs. Yates's water flowed freely from the ground! Truly a gift from God!

The pièce de résistance or finale to the summer visits came with the watermelon feast. My father would go to the grocery store and pick out a giant green watermelon. He could tell if the melon was sufficiently ripe by thumping on it with his knuckle—a gift my cousin Bonnie says that she possesses except that she somehow thumps on her toe and compares that sound to the sound made when the watermelon is thumped! The watermelon would be stored in the milk cooler down by the barn until it was ice cold. Remember, all of this happened before the days of central air-conditioning, and August was usually the hottest month. So, as the final feast of summer, all of the relatives and cousins would gather at our house, and my father would split open the ripe watermelon, and we kids ate till we could eat no more. My father would seriously discuss with my aunts and uncles if he had picked the right melon at its peak of ripeness, but to us children, it really didn't matter. They were all sweet and juicy and better still, ice cold!

CHAPTER 8
PERMANENCE AS A WAY OF LIFE

On the farm, very few things were ever done on a temporary basis. There were never enough hours in the day or enough energy in one's body to do the same job a second time. But I do remember that we had a corn crib that was located near the barn, which was always referred to as the "temporary" corn crib. It had a wooden floor, perhaps forty feet long and about five feet wide, with upright wooden posts, perhaps fifteen feet high to support the tin roof, with some cross pieces for bracing, and then the sides of the structure were covered with heavy wire fencing to hold in the ears of corn. The passage of the air through the fencing helped the corn to further dry before it was removed from the crib to be shelled, and then it was ground up for use in the animal feed.

One spring in 1954 when I was a freshman in high school, a storm came along and the wind blew this corn crib over. It was empty at this time of year. So my father began to make plans for a "permanent" corn crib. We laughed as my mother recounted that the temporary corn crib had served its purpose for seventeen years and we frequently joked about it. But in the following year, the joke was soon to be on brother John and I as my father rolled out his plans for a permanent corn storage facility. I do not remember seeing any plans for that corn crib as I suspect that those plans resided mostly in my father's head!

My father's plans for a permanent corn storage facility called for a building about thirty-five feet long and at least twenty feet wide. There would be two cribs on either side whose width would be about five feet, with an eight-foot walkway in the center, which would allow air to circulate to the corn on the inside. The corn was also to be stored over the top of the walkway to a depth of about five feet. The building was constructed of rough sawn hardwood. The outside of the building was covered with horizontal slats of hardwood, separated by about half an inch to allow the air to circulate. The slats were about an inch and a half wide but, instead of being sawn with square edges, the edges of the slats were slanted so that, when it rained, the water would run to the outside of the crib, away from the corn.

The entire structure was to be built on a concrete foundation. As is taught in the Bible, "a foolish man builds his house upon the sand, while the wise man builds his house upon a rock!" And so my brother John and I began to dig the foundation for this "permanent" corn crib under the hot August summer sun in 1955. The foundation consisted of four, thirty-five foot-long walls. These walls were to be dug deep enough so that the frost would never reach the bottom of the foundation. And to my father's way of thinking, the outside walls needed to be at least five feet deep and the inside walls were to be at least four feet deep. And so, with shovel, pick, maddox, and wheelbarrow, we began digging. And we dug, and dug, and dug. At the end of the day, I didn't have enough strength in my arms to wheel the wheelbarrow of dirt to the pile in the field just west of the construction site, and my brother John would have to wheel the loads himself. And when we would ask if we had dug the foundation deep enough, my father would say no, he didn't want the frost to crack and heave the foundation. He said that he wanted the outside walls of the foundation to be deep enough so that the handle of the shovel would disappear when stood vertically in the hole. And so we kept digging until he was satisfied. Next came the chore of mixing all of the concrete that was needed to fill the foundation forms. And this was no small task, either, as I think my father finally realized that we had really dug ourselves into a big hole, so to speak. Truckload after truckload of sand and gravel were delivered. And each day we would mix more concrete. And when it looked like we had run out of concrete, my father directed us to take the tractor and wagon and gather up all of the stones that had been collected from the fields. (When the fields were plowed, an occasional stone would show up and, usually, one picked up the stone and discarded it onto a pile at the end of the field.) And so we hauled load after load of stones and brought them to the construction site to be entombed into the concrete we were mixing. And as each stone was dropped into the foundation, care was taken to make sure that each stone was encapsulated with fresh wet concrete. This we did until all of the stone piles around the farm had been used up! And when we finished, we had a magnificent foundation, capable of holding hundreds of tons of corn, withstanding countless winters of freezing and thawing temperatures, and perhaps, a direct hit from an atomic bomb!

My father supervised the construction of the wooden structure. It was one of the last times that I remember seeing my Grandfather Fred Yoder come over to help nail on the wood slats. As I recall, the structure was finally finished in time for the new crop of corn. And we used an elevator and gravity box wagons to fill the crib from holes cut in the metal roof. All of our hard work had finally paid off as the wagons could now be unloaded without shoveling!

Storing corn on the cob is something that is no longer done by most farmers today, since the modern combines shell the corn in the field and deposits the cobs and fodder back onto the fields. But my father knew that storing the corn on the cobs was the lowest cost way to store corn and resulted in a better product due to the fact that the kernels of corn keep taking nutrients from the cob long after the ear is picked. And, of course, drying the corn was done by natural circulation of the air around the ears of corn, not by using huge metals bins that have to be heated by expensive propane gas to dry the kernels sufficiently enough to keep them from spoiling. When the corn was needed in the winter to feed the animals, it was unloaded from the crib and taken to the mill to be ground up and mixed with other grains and fed to the cows.

And corn was not just used as animal feed on the farm, either. We would dry some corn in the house over the hot air registers and then take the corn to a mill in Creston, Ohio, to be shelled and then ground into flour. Stone grinding is best as the nutrients in the kernels are not destroyed from the heat of stone grist mills. This corn meal would be our winter "cereal" for the family. My mother would cook a big iron kettle of corn meal mush on the stove and serve corn meal mush for supper on a cold winter night. Usually, the corn meal mush was eaten with fresh milk and syrup. The remainder of the mush would be poured into a pan to be cooled for later use. My mother would slice the cooled mush into about one-inch-thick slabs. The slabs of mush would be fried in a cast iron skillet using lard as the shortening of choice, which gave the mush a beautiful light brown crust. When served with maple syrup, it made a wonderful breakfast! I can remember being made fun of at school for having corn meal mush for breakfast. But we are just awakening to the nutritional benefits of eating whole grain cereals.

CHAPTER 9

THE WINDS OF CHANGE

In December of 1957 during my senior year in high school, my brother John left the farm for military service in the army. And so it became my turn to get up early in the morning around 5:00 a.m. to help with milking the cows before school began. Usually breakfast was around 7:00 a.m. and then the bus would come around 7:30 a.m. and I would be off to school. I would return from school sometime around four that afternoon, and it would be time to start the evening chores. Supper was at six-thirty, and then there would be a little time for me to do any necessary homework and then off to bed to rest for the next day. I maintained this schedule during my senior year in high school as well as playing trumpet in the marching band and being a member of the debate team.

By this time in my life, I was dating and had a girlfriend whom I really liked and wanted to spend time with. I remember one summer Saturday evening when we finished combining wheat in the field at 10:00 p.m. (this was a hot, dusty job as I hauled the wheat into the barn and shoveled it into the granary while my father ran the combine). I rushed back to the house, took a quick bath, dressed, and went over to her house, probably arriving around 11:00 p.m. After almost falling asleep while at her house, she sent me home. It was a wise move on her part, since I knew I would have to get up the next morning at five to milk the cows and to go to church!

After I graduated from high school, this relationship became more serious. But it also started to come apart as I became torn between wanting this relationship and also knowing that my mother was counting on me to go to college. I had already decided to follow in my mother's footsteps and attend Manchester College in North Manchester Indiana. And besides, I had no money or any particular skills to earn money other than working on a farm. And I had already decided that farming was not for me and that further education was my only opportunity to learn how to support myself. My mother wanted me to become a preacher, but that vocation did not seem to lie in the direction I wanted to go. Still, one fact remained perfectly clear to me: attending college was my only chance to become "successful."

And so in the fall of 1958, I left the only life that I had ever known and a girl that I truly loved, broken hearted and homesick, never to return. Yes, I would come back during college breaks, and during the first summer recess, but I would never return to become a part of the farm again, only as a visiting family member.

After I retired, Jeanette and I moved to Canandaigua, NY. We built a new home on the east side of Canandaigua Lake that overlooks the lake. We love the quietness of the country, the clean air, the Canadian geese and ducks that make the lake their home, as well as all of the deer and wild animals that come to the lake for water. We discovered the Finger Lakes Region of New York during our courtship, as we often came to Watkins Glen in the summer for dinner on Saturday night and to enjoy Seneca Lake afterwards. I also enjoyed visiting the many wineries that surround the Finger Lakes Region and thought that this area could potentially be a nice place to spend my retirement years. On one fine spring day, Jeanette and I met my son Michael, his wife Michelle, and their son Christian for lunch at the Canandaigua Inn. For a retirement gift, Michael gave us two tickets for lunch on the Canandaigua Lady (a replica, split paddle-wheel steamboat), and a little later I decided that we all should go. Jeanette fell in love with the City of Canandaigua and so began the idea of living here in Canandaigua. We came again to Canandaigua late that summer and stayed at a B&B along East Lake Road. The lady there recommended that we take a look at the "Deep Run Development" just down the road. And in less than a year, we were moving into our new home!

I draw a great deal of pleasure in looking at all of the farms that are in the area. The land is not very well drained, and sometimes the weather can be harsh, but a great deal of milk, vegetables, grapes, and fruits are produced in the Finger Lakes Region of New York. There are huge "corporate farms" with hundreds of dairy cows that never go out into the fields to dine on the fresh grass as all of the feed is brought to them; nursery farms that raise nothing but calves, which will later either be sold for veal or to yet another farm, which will feed them until they become heifers, which will be bred and then sold again to the dairy farms as milk cows; there are egg factories, which house thousands and thousands of chickens in steel cages, never to see the sun or to scratch in the earth for a worm or bug. I smell the dank stench of the corporate farms as they haul their liquid manure from the manure pits onto the fields with huge 10,000-gallon honey wagons. The liquid is so strong that it kills all vegetation and nothing can be planted in that soil for another six weeks. I watch the giant John Deere tractors that have four wheels on the front, four wheels on the back that make only a humming sound as they plow the earth and prepare the ground for planting. I watch the harvesting machines in the fall and winter as they combine the soybeans and the corn, cutting two-foot deep ruts in the soft wet earth.

But, there are other kinds of farms in the Finger Lakes area. These are farms that I am more familiar with. They are owned and operated by the Amish and Mennonites that have moved into the area. Some of the farms are still farmed by horse, but the majority of them use steel-wheeled tractors. Not the skinny steel wheels that one might see on an antique 1939 Farmall tractor, but giant steel wheels that are perhaps two or three feet wide. You see, the land can be worked much earlier with these tractors than it can be with an ordinary rubber tired tractor, since the rubber tired tractor would sink hopelessly into the mud. And yes, they have steel-wheeled Bobcats that they use to clean out the manure in their barns and steel-wheeled John Deere lawn tractors to mow the grass around their homes! Some of these "plain folks" have come to rebuild the old homes and broken down barns that exist in the area. Some have come to build anew. Each farm also has a second business—perhaps a greenhouse, a saw mill, a roofing business, or a vegetable farm. Much of their produce, crafts, and flowers can be seen at the Windmill, a huge outdoor market located between Pen Yann and Dundee, New York. It is only open on Saturdays as these folks are farmers, not merchants. Jeanette marvels at the taste of fresh organically grown strawberries, beans, corn, tomatoes, potatoes, squash, and meat that we purchase at the Windmill. As for me and my way of thinking, that is what meat and produce are supposed to taste like!

On a summer evening, I love to ride my motorcycle down Route 364 to Pen Yann. It's easy to spot the farms run by the "plain folks." First, you can tell by all of the flowers planted around the house. My mother loved flowers and so do these folks. Flowers take a lot of work, but around their homes, it almost becomes a statement of thankfulness and praise to God for the sun and rain that allows them to make their living. There, on the left, is a farm with a greenhouse and beautiful flowers all around the house. The calves and heifers are out in their separate pastures, enjoying a late evening snack of grass. Further down the road on the right, a new farm has sprung up just a little uphill from the site of the old fallen down buildings. The house has a green metal roof and a covered porch that wraps itself all around the house. The barn is new also and it too has a green metal roof. There are horses in the pasture. I start to pick up speed as I begin to go down a long winding hill. On the left there are beautiful fields, first a strip of corn, and then a strip of hay, then another strip of corn, and then one of wheat. My father would have loved to see these fields! These people farm just as he did. Not a weed to be seen at the end of the rows! The fields are a blur now as I descend into the valley and then start to climb back up to the top of the hill on the other side of the valley. As I come up over the crest of the hill, I slow down a bit.

On the left is a produce farm, and I see a women with an apron on, bent over at her waist, picking some of the fresh green beans. She reminds me of my mother as she toils in her garden, and I want to stop and ask her how the tomatoes are doing or when the sweet corn will be ready. But I ride on.

We were having dinner at the Essen House restaurant near Pen Yann with Jeanette's daughter Susan and her grandson Colin one summer Sunday evening. As we were eating, we saw a group of young Amish people riding their bicycles past the restaurant. And then the older folks passed by in their horse drawn buggies. I explained to Colin that these people were on their way to church and that they do not drive motor-driven, rubber-tired vehicles on the road and that they farm either with horses or with steel-wheeled tractors. Colin looked at me and said, "Why would anybody want to live like that?" I didn't answer.

Perhaps we need to ask ourselves the same question: "Why would anyone want to live the way we live?"

James R. Bupp

ADDENDUM
CHIPPEWA CHURCH OF THE
BRETHREN HISTORY WRITTEN
BY DONNA REHM IN 2005

Chippewa Church of the Brethren was first started in 1868. At least that was when the first building was put up. They met in barns and homes before that. It covered a large area from Akron and to the south. And in May 29, 1877, the church was divided up into congregations, including Orville, Wooster, and Chippewa. At that time there were 131 members. The first council meeting held after the division in the Chippewa congregation was August 18, 1877, with Elder George Irvin in Charge. The first love feast was held in the Beech Groove House September 20, 1885. In 1910, necessity required that something be done with the church house, and it was decided to build new. This church house was sent for in the *Sears and Roebuck Catalog* and was shipped by rail to Sterling, Ohio, and brought to the present site by wagons and teams of horses. There was no basement under the old church. So the men of the church used teams and hand-held scoops to dig out for the basement under the new church house. The extra dirt was put on the south side of the church lot, since it was low there. Dedication was held July 28, 1912, with the church full and one hundred people standing outside. September 7, 1912, at 10:00 a.m., the first Love Feast was held in the present building. January 1, 1914, the membership of the Chippewa congregation was 212. My father told me stories of the Love Feast when the neighbors close to the church came and sat in the pews and watched our congregation wash feet. The communion room was in the narthex area and large doors separated that room from the auditorium. The Communion room would be full as people from the area churches, including Paradise, Akron, and Mohican would come to communion with us. They would come by horse and buggy and would stay in the church over night. That was before the world of TV and other activities took over.

There were two men who served the church as free ministers. Their names were Simon Showalter and

Claude Murray. Showalter was a farmer, and Murray had a traveling grocery business, to support them. They took turns preaching. As a child, I remember Showalter as a very loud speaker with excitement in his voice. And Murray was a very quiet speaker who never raised his voice. As of July 21, 1926–1930, a man by the name of A. Gale Freed was our first part-time paid Pastor.

In 1927, a Delco-Light Plant was installed in our church for $350.00 less battery. It was 1928 before the congregation voted to install a musical instrument in the church. There was much discussion over a piano in the church. In fact, there were about 25 people left the church at that time. It was known that some of these people played musical instruments in their homes, including guitars, fiddles, and pianos, and they even played for barn dances.

Trees were planted around the cemetery in 1933. This was a gift of Flora Hoff. A cemetery lot is free to all members of the Chippewa Church; only a fee for opening and closing the grave is asked. Just ask the sexton about a spot.

There were horse and buggy sheds to house the horses people drove to church, on the West Side of the church all the way along the back. These sheds were torn down as they were no longer in use by 1936. Only a couple was left on the north side of the church to take care of Daniel Shafer's horse and buggy. That would have been Dan Shafer's Great Grandfather. Earl Miller bought evergreen trees from the Shook Lumber Company in Rittman. At that time, there were fifty-four evergreens planted across the back of the church. They were bought for fifty cents apiece already dug and bagged. The men of the church planted them. Another double row of pine trees were placed back farther at the edge of the lot at a later time. Paul Lehman (father of June Lehman) gave many of those trees to the church.

Roland Showalter came to preach every other Sunday for three months. That was 1938. A Rev. S.P. Early was hired on a full-time basis in 1939. Then we hired Rev. Paul Shrider part time in 1944. Rev. David Landis was hired full time and later allowed to work in 1948. In 1948, every member was given a silver Dollar to invest for the parsonage fund. The return for that project was

$822.69. It was in 1953 that Rev. Robert Winkler was hired and, in 1954, the men of the church built the new Parsonage. Pastor Winkler moved into the new parsonage. The dedication of the parsonage took place on August 8, 1954.

The youth of the church at one time raised money to send two heifers overseas through the Heifer Project. They mowed the church lawn and cemetery and other projects to make money to buy these animals. Also, several farmers at the church sent bulls and heifers.

The Everybody Welcome Sunday School class in the church took a refugee family (Emanuel May, his wife, and six Children) to sponsor in an Austria camp. They sent them food, clothing, and household items. Then the family wanted to come to the USA, and they had some relatives already here. So the Class asked the church to help them sponsor the family. In August 1955, the May Family was brought to our community. In 1962, our church also sponsored a man named Naum Karbatak also from Yugoslavia, and then we sponsored a family from Viet Nam. Their name was Vuong. There was a family of nine in this group. A new baby was born to the younger couple while still with us. These people and families were brought to us through Brethren Service in New Windsor, Maryland.

Rev. Ted Gandy was hired as our pastor in 1955. We had the Carr Associates come into our church for a fund raising campaign. This was a three-year program to raise $10,000.00 to obtain finances for the regular expenses and also for remodeling the church, which took place in 1957.

The church was remodeled in 1958. The basement wall was taken out and a new wall and windows were put in all around the church basement. No more snakes in the basement! All the old blocks from the basement wall were taken and put down in the parking lot north of the church to give it a firm foundation. More room was dug out for the men and women's restrooms to be put in the basement. Up to this time we had nothing but outside toilets. Our men at the church did most all of the work in the evening hours after they had worked all day. The women of the church took turns bringing snacks for the men each evening. Everyone put in long, hard hours, but we had a nice basement when it was finished. The upstairs Sunday school classrooms were also built at that time. The large doors leading to the communion room were removed and the narthex was made with a nice entrance, as we now know it. The little room in the tower was torn down, as was the tower. Pictures of these buildings can be seen on the narthex wall. The Dedication Service for the remodeling was held on July 26, 1959. New carpet was put in the Sanctuary. An addition was built onto the stage in the front of the sanctuary at a later date.

We had our Pastor Rev. Dean Kindy in 1960, Rev. Tim Monn, in 1979, Ted and Betty Young, who were voted in on June 29, 1981. Ted Young died in 1985, Betty stayed with us until Dec. 1992. Randal Lehman served as our interim Pastor until Pastor Doug Wantz came in 1993.

Made in the USA
Charleston, SC
16 February 2010